What makes *The 40-Day Surren̶d̶e̶r̶* ̶
doesn't merely require absten̶
directed to surrender whatever ̶
with God. For me, that wa̶
accustomed to entertaining n̶ ̶ ̶ ̶ ̶ ̶ ̶ ̶ ̶ ̶ ̶were
contrary to the way God viewed ̶ ̶ ̶ ̶ ̶ ̶through the process of
surrender was difficult, the daily devotions and encouragement
from others enabled me to renew my mind. To this day I
reference the surrender fast when I need to be reminded that I
can do all things through Christ.

–VANESSA S.

This is the craziest, most rewarding fast I have ever done! I
thought I was simply surrendering my favorite smoothie, but
by the end of the fast I learned I had surrendered my will. By
God's grace I died to myself and was lifted from the dungeons
of self-abasement and self-reliance. Now instead of "sitting" in
faith, I recline in faith with my feet totally off the ground.
Because I surrendered, God is now the source of all my
expectations.

–LESLIE D.

The 40-Day Surrender Fast transformed my life. While fasting
one of my long-standing prayer request was answered—I
started teaching as an adjunct professor at a local university!
Also during that time I was blessed to adapt *The 40-Day
Surrender Fast* model for over 300 volunteers at a jail ministry.
Together we did an 8-day "mini" surrender fast with the hopes

that God would elevate the ministry. Day by day, we saw the jail ministry being transformed and lives being blessed. For these and many other reasons, I am so grateful for this fast. Because of it I have a clearer vision and stronger determination to fulfill God's perfect plan.

—SYLVIA H.

I was intrigued by the idea of a *40-Day Surrender Fast* but unsure why or if I should do it. So I sought the Lord and He directed me to surrender my heart. I've had my share of heart problems—a heart attack in 1993 and double bypass heart surgery in 2001. As a result I made significant lifestyle changes, but God wanted more. *"You're working to obtain a healthy 'physical' heart but I want your HEART!"* I then knew why *The 40-Day Surrender Fast* was necessary. During the course of fasting the Lord ministered His wants and desires. Accordingly, I am allowing His perfect plan to unfold for my life.

–WANDA J.

I am in total awe of what God did in 40 days! As I fasted from television something major happened. Four years ago I started taking medication for sleep and quickly became addicted. During the fast as I spent more time with God, He became my peace, and I started falling asleep without the medication. On the last day of *The 40-Day Surrender Fast* I flushed all the pills down the toilet. I am completely delivered because I surrender my will for His.

–KIMBERLY A.

THE
40-DAY

———

SURRENDER
FAST

The Guide for Releasing Your Plan,
Renewing Your Mind, and Restoring Your Life

Celeste Owens, Ph.D.

Good Success
Publishing

Good Success Publishing

The 40-Day Surrender Fast
©2011 by Celeste Owens.

This book is also available as an ebook.
Visit www.surrenderfast.com.

Requests for information should be addressed to:
Good Success Publishing,
P.O. Box 134, Oxon Hill, MD 20750-0134

ISBN: 978-0-9837895-0-5 (softcover)

Library of Congress Control Number: 2011933636

This book is printed on acid-free paper.

Cover design: Pixel Ink Studios
Interior design: YAV Publications
Printed in the United States of America

Second printing

Tonya!
Enjoy!
Stephanie

This book is dedicated to
the 100+ bloggers who dared to surrender.

God bless
Dr. Celeste

Contents

Acknowledgements

To God: Thank you for allowing me to be on the most awesome journey with You. I know the best is yet to come.

To Andel: Thank you for your love, patience, and unfailing support. When God created you, He knew just what I needed and I am so grateful.

To Andel Jr. and Aaliyah: What amazing creations you are. I pray that you live fully surrendered to God and fulfill the call He has on your lives.

To Donald and Malinda Chisholm: You are the best parents a girl could have. Thank you for living a life of integrity and demonstrating unwavering faith in the midst of your challenges. Your love and support throughout the years has made me who I am today.

To my church family (First Baptist Church of Glenarden): What a blessing you all have been to me. A special thanks to *Pastor John K. Jenkins, Sr.* and *First Lady Trina Jenkins.* It has been a pleasure following your godly examples of humility and excellence. Thank you for all that you do to support this ministry. Additional thanks to *Minister Willie Jolley* who encouraged me to self-publish; *Allison Johnson* who coined the term "surrender fast"; and *Michelle Singletary* who took a chance on me and exposed me to unchartered waters.

To my sisters Brandy and Nicole: What a journey this has been. Thanks for joining me every Monday for our weekly prayer. Because of that time this was made possible. *Andrea:* Thank you for lending your expertise in the area of logo design. I never knew that you were so creative. *Chanelle:* Thank you for your encouragement and spontaneous tears of joy. *Latricia:* Thank you for believing in this work and for all our long "destiny" conversations.

To my brothers Don Jr., Jason, and Stephen: Each of you, in your own way, influenced the content of this book and we are richer for it.

To my "editors": Candyce Anderson, Tonya Brewington, Tanya Bryant, Yaphet Bryant, Chanelle Chisholm, Latricia Chisholm, Gina Davis, Stephanie Davis, Sylvia Huntley, Tyra Kingsland, Wanda Scales, and Yolanda Simpson. Thank you for all of your help!

To Chris: Thank you for lending your publishing expertise. May God continue to bless YAV Publications.

To Carolyn, Jonesie, Kim, and Stephanie: Thank you for all the encouragement. Our little book club has made a big difference in my life.

INTRODUCTION

In the fall of 2010, approximately 100 people joined me in corporate fasting. This wasn't your typical fast—a little quirky in fact, but it was the fast that God had ordained. Therefore, in obedience to Him we "surrendered."

I wasn't new to this process; in fact, the 2010 blogged fast marked my third 40-day fast that year. The first time I surrendered certain types of food. For years the Holy Spirit had been convicting me about my eating habits. Although I knew the importance of a proper nutrition, having read many books concerning diet and healthy eating, I continue to eat foods that didn't edify my body. However, (by God's grace) in the early part of 2010 I eliminated every unhealthy food from my diet for 40 days and He performed a miracle. You'll hear more about that transformation in later sections of this book.

My second fast was from "selfishness." I vowed that for 40 days I would serve my family without complaint and with a heart of joy. It wasn't easy, but through daily prayer, reading of the Bible and other Christian books my heart changed and my family truly became my first priority.

My third and final 40-day fast of 2010 was blogged from September 6–October 22. The following devotional is the fruit of that fast. Those who finished were blessed tremendously.

I was so excited about what God had done for us that I started telling others and they, too, completed the fast and like us, they were immensely blessed. All participants reported that the fast had been just as relevant for them as it had been for us, despite the time differential. That's when I knew this gift from God needed to be shared with many more people.

The content of what you are about to read is for the most part unedited. I felt it was important that you read God's words just as He gave them to us.

I pray that like us, you have an experience with God that exceeds all other encounters with Him and that the benefits of your surrender are reaped for many generations to come. I am a witness that this fast, if followed faithfully and honestly, will change your life. So without further ado, welcome to the Surrender Fast.

IS THIS REALLY A FAST?

In the Hebrew the word for fast is "sum" and means to voluntarily abstain from food as dedication to deity. Today, most religious fasting consists of an absolute or partial abstention from food for a specified amount of time. As a matter of fact, I am big proponent of this form of fasting as I have been a recipient of its benefits.

However, in this book fasting is approached differently; one is simply asked to surrender or abstain from something dear for 40 days. While unconventional, this way of fasting produces results. Many of those who have participated in this fast—whether veteran fasters or novice—

reported deliverance from their strongholds, renewed faith, and a closer, more intimate relationship with God.

I am not suggesting that the Surrender Fast is to replace traditional fasting but I am proposing that they both have their place. In Isaiah 58:6-9a, God says that He will produce the results we seek, when we fast in the manner that pleases Him:

> "Is this not the fast that I have chosen:
> To loose the bonds of wickedness,
> To undo the heavy burdens,
> To let the oppressed go free,
> And that you break every yoke?
>
> Then your light shall break forth like the morning,
> Your healing shall spring forth speedily,
> And your righteousness shall go before you;
> The glory of the LORD shall be your rear guard.
>
> Then you shall call, and the LORD will answer;
> You shall cry, and He will say, 'Here I am.'"

What a wonderful promise from the Lord. When we fast according to His will, He hears our prayer, draws closer to us, and attends to our needs.

FASTING GUIDELINES

Here are a few guidelines to assist you in successfully completing this fast:

1. **Seek God for guidance.** Pray and ask God what He would have you surrender for the next 40 days. By way of example, some have fasted from selfishness, junk food, fear, television, secular music, and/or envy.

2. **Read the Pre-Fast Preparation section.** Ideally these posts should be read one per day for at least 5 days prior to the start of your fast. However, they could be read two per day or all in one sitting. No matter your method of choice, be sure to meditate on each passage and journal what you sense God is saying to you.

3. **Begin the 40-day fast.** Start Day 1 on a Monday. Begin each day with prayer, the reading of the Word, and this devotional. There is a devotional for each weekday. Be sure to answer the Personal Reflection questions at the end of each post which are designed to further engage you in the process. Also, read scriptures that are related to your area of surrender. For example, if you are abstaining from negative talk, read scriptures relating to the tongue, complaining, gossiping, idle talk, etc. Lastly, use the weekend to read whatever God lays on your heart and journal.

4. **Ask a friend to fast with you.** It helps to have another person or persons available for accountability and encouragement. Most people who have taken this fast have done so with at least one other person.

5. **Enjoy the journey.** Don't be too hard on yourself during the 40 days. A closer walk with God, not perfection is the goal. Therefore, seek Him with all your heart, surrender your will for His, and watch Him do the miraculous in your life.

Let God Do a New Thing!

You may be wondering, "What is Celeste up to now?" I'm not up to anything, it's God. In the next few days He will call you to do something you hadn't considered and subsequently redirect the course of your life.

As some of you know, I have been home all year. At the close of 2009 God called me to leave all that I knew—private practice, speaking, writing, ministry duties—to go to a place He would disclose. I soon discovered that the undisclosed location was my house!

So at the top of 2010, I found myself home with two little ones and plenty of time to be with God. I must admit I questioned God's plan at first, but as I look back over the last nine months I am thankful that He redirected the course of my life and changed me in ways quite unexpected. Now He wants to do the same for you.

God is calling you to do something different—to move out of your comfort zone. Don't resist and don't let fear keep you from what He has in store. Isaiah 43:18-19 reads:

> Do not remember the former things,
> Nor consider the things of old.

Behold, I will do a new thing,
Now it shall spring forth;
Shall you not know it?
I will even make a road in the wilderness
And rivers in the desert.

Yes, God can and will do all that for you.

What is the secret desire of your heart? He knows, but won't move without your full cooperation and a complete surrender of your will. And that's where this fast comes in. In the next week, because you are seeking change, you are going to surrender some habit or belief to God for 40 days. We will start the journey together this Monday.

I have done two 40-day fasts since April. Each time with other people (i.e., corporate fasting) and we have been miraculously changed. This time God has called me to do it with you via blog. I will explain more tomorrow.

Les Brown says, "If you want to make this your decade, you've got to decide to be bold, to take life on." Don't leave the year the same way you came in. The former things have passed; God wants to do a new thing in you.

Personal Reflections

1. How is the Spirit speaking to you? Reflect on Isaiah 43:18-19 and journal your insights.

2. What "new thing" does God want to do in and for you?

3. Like Dr. Celeste, do you sense that God is asking you to give up some tasks or jobs that are important to you? Will you comply?

4. What role, if any, will fear play in hindering you from allowing God to do the new thing in your life?

What is a Surrender Fast?

A ccording to the Merriam-Webster Dictionary, to surrender is to give oneself up into the power of another, especially as a prisoner. Likewise, when one is arrested what's the first thing that he does? He raises his hands in an act of surrender and submits to the authority of a higher power. That type of surrender—releasing your will and plan in favor of God's—is what this fast is all about.

I am near completion of a book that I believe will change the way this generation approaches success. It outlines the steps that every person must take to fulfill his/her destiny. The fifth step on this journey is "Isolation" and the proper conclusion to this stage is a fast. Jesus modeled this or us. During His time of isolation in the wilderness, He fasted for 40 days and nights from food and drink (Matthew 4:1-11). As a reward for his complete surrender to God's plan, He was ushered into His destiny. I formulated this fast, and subsequently named it *The 40-Day Surrender Fast*, based on Jesus' time of fasting in the wilderness.

My first experience with the Surrender Fast was in April of 2010. While attending a women's fellowship at the

First Baptist Church of Glenarden, Pastor John K. Jenkins Sr. taught on the disciplines of a godly woman. I was instantly convicted about my lack of discipline in the area of diet. For many years God had been dealing with me about my eating habits. Even as a 3-year survivor of breast cancer I was content to eat what I liked, despite my knowledge of the link between diet and disease. I was so controlled by food that I was willing to hinder my physical and spiritual health for the momentary thrill of a box of Hot Tamales! I knew that God wasn't pleased and I was desperate for a change.

So on that Saturday morning in April I cried. And when my crying had ended, I decided to do what God had been instructing me to do for years. I surrendered my will for His in this area.

I chose to do the Daniel Fast. During my time of fasting I shared my testimony with other women and a few of them joined me. Each of us fasted from something different, one from TV, another sugar, but our hearts were in concert together as we collectively surrendered our wills. Initially, the fast was difficult for me, but somewhere around day 31, and much to my surprise, I decided to become a vegetarian and I haven't looked back since.

So now it's your turn. If you are feeling stuck, frustrated, and/or bound decide that now is the time to do something new; have the courage to release your plan for His. The blessings that will stem from your obedience will be well worth the sacrifice (see Deuteronomy 28).

Personal Reflections

1. How is the Spirit speaking to you? Reflect on Matthew 4:1-11 and journal your insights.

2. Dr. Celeste was introduced to fasting as a child and has continued the practice into adulthood. However, some new or even seasoned converts for that matter don't regard fasting as beneficial. What are your thoughts about fasting? Have you fasted in the past and did it produce the results you expected? What do you expect from this fast?

3. What area(s) of your life do you need to surrender to God? What will be most challenging about surrendering?

4. How might this surrender change your relationship with yourself, God, and others?

Bold and Courageous

*C*eleste, just as I instructed Joshua, 'Be bold and courageous' is what God has been urging all year. In an effort to make this command my truth, I have read and re-read the book of Joshua. It has changed me tremendously, but there is still more that God wants to do. That's the reason He has called me to this fast (and dragged you in with me); I need to be released. I can no longer allow the hurts of the past to dictate my actions and keep me from being bold and courageous. He needs me to be an ambassador of His word and if I am timid and shy I won't be an effective witness.

My lack of boldness came to a head the other day. I was helping a candidate solicit votes at a polling site. While there, I ran into a colleague who was campaigning for a different candidate. After a few pleasantries we got into a conversation about the candidates that were running for office that term. She disagreed, quite vehemently, with those I sought to support and sought to change my mind.

Suffice it to say, it worked. By the time she was done I had changed one of my votes. To make matters worse, I looked for her after I voted to let her know that I had been persuaded by her argument. Fortunately I couldn't get her approval; she had left the site. I realized immediately that that interaction had been a set up. God had my attention.

I relay this embarrassing story to highlight my need for God—especially in this area. Last night I prayed for insight into my behavior. God revealed to me that I lose myself when I am around aggressive/assertive people; I don't feel empowered to appropriately handle their type.

The root of the problem dates back to grade school. I desperately wanted to fit in, but didn't. I was continuously rejected by (at least in my mind) the aggressive, sometimes mean, yet overwhelmingly popular "it" girls.

At the same time, I was overly invested in pleasing my authority figures believing, in error, that their approval would make me good and acceptable. All lies. God's acceptance of me is all that matters.

I am learning day by day that He loves me just the way I am. As I grow closer to Him, I gain the courage to be just who I am. Before this year is out I will be firm in my identity, sure of my calling, and ready for any and every assignment that comes my way. Because of Christ and the work that He did for me on the cross, I am whole and complete in God.

I read this morning, "Do not fear, for you will not be ashamed; Neither be disgraced, for you will not be put to shame; For you will forget the shame of your youth," (Isaiah 54:4a). He was reminding me that I am not that scared little girl who had no voice and needed acceptance. I am a bold and courageous woman in Christ. I am also reminded that God will give us double for our trouble (see Isaiah 61:7) and make up for all of the hurts we have experienced.

We will boldly declare this day, that we are healed from the pains and wounds of the past; we are new in Christ, and equipped to succeed in all that we put our hands to. So for the next 40 days, starting Monday, September 13, I am fasting from a timid and fearful attitude, especially as it relates to aggressive/assertive people. I will speak as the Spirit leads and I will not let fear shut me down. What will you surrender to God?

Personal Reflections

1. How is the Spirit speaking to you? Reflect on Isaiah 54:3-6 and journal your insights.

2. Have you decided what you will surrender for the next 40 days? If yes, write it below. If not, don't worry. Just continue to seek God's direction and He will give you the answer. Like Dr. Celeste who was encouraged by the words God spoke to Joshua, how has God prepared your heart for such a fast?

3. The enemy wants you to be ashamed of your weaknesses and to hide them from others, but that philosophy only delays your healing. Therefore, identify a weakness and write what that is below. Make arrangements to talk with at least one other person about it. Ask him/her to hold you accountable (through the duration of the fast) as you allow God to change you in this area.

4. If you can't readily identify a person that can be part of this process with you, pray. God will reveal the right person to you. When He does go to that person, explain what you are doing, and ask them to be part of this journey with you. List the name of that person here.

Why 40 Days?

The number forty is significant for several reasons. One, it is universally accepted as a number of importance to God not only for the frequency of its occurrence in the Bible but also for its association with a period of trial and probation. For example:

- In Noah's day the rains fell for 40 days and nights (Genesis 7:4)
- The children of Israel wandered the wilderness for 40 years (Joshua 5:6)
- Goliath presented himself to Israel for 40 days (1 Samuel 17:16)
- David reigned over Israel for 40 years (2 Samuel 5:4; 1 Kings 2:11)
- Jesus fasted 40 days and 40 nights (Matthew 4:2)
- Jesus was tempted 40 days (Luke 4:2; Mark 1:14)

And just as an aside, women are pregnant for 40 weeks.

Secondly, the number 40 is significant because it appears to be, at least from my experiences, the right amount of time needed to break a stronghold. You may have read, and research indicates that it takes about 21 days to make or break a habit. This may be true, but a stronghold is something different; it's a habit gone wild. In the spiritual a stronghold is an incorrect pattern of thinking that influences how we live our lives. For that reason, 40 days appears to be the more accurate number for breaking a stronghold.

Strongholds can be evident in many areas of our lives, but one area where they can be especially detrimental is in our emotional life. After years of hurt, we naturally seek to protect our emotions. In a futile attempt to ward off further pain, we often adopt incorrect beliefs (e.g., people will always hurt me so I shouldn't let anyone get too close). These erroneous beliefs don't allow us to move as God instructs and keep us from taking the risks that are necessary for success.

In and of ourselves we are hopeless to change, but with God all things are possible. His healing virtue tears down the walls that have kept us confined and His grace propels us further than we ever thought we could go.

This is my third time doing this particular 40-day fast (the first time I fasted from certain types of foods and the second from the pride and selfishness). Each time I noticed a distinct pattern. The first 21 days were challenging, I couldn't see how God was going to change me. Right around day 21, I started sensing that change was on the way. About day 30, I started noticing consistent changes in my behavior. And by day 40, I was healed; a new me restored and renewed in mind, body, and spirit.

The scripture reminds us that some things only change through prayer and fasting (see Mark 9:29). Are you ready to be free and released from your stronghold? If so, this is your time of probation; your chance to prove to God and yourself that you are ready to accept the new thing that He has for you. Commit yourself to this fast and see God do a mighty work in your life.

Personal Reflections

1. *How is the Spirit speaking to you?* Reflect on Mark 9:14-29 and journal your insights.

2. What behaviors or circumstances keep you bound and also act as a barrier to the life God has for you?

3. Do you believe that God can deliver you from any and every stronghold? Think of a behavior or habit that you would like to eliminate. What have you tried in the past to rid yourself of this problem? Has the problem gotten better over time or remained the same? How will you know when God has healed you?

4. Are you willing to commit to this period of fasting for 40 days? What people or circumstances might negatively impact your ability to succeed at this fast?

It's Complicated

Within the "Info" section of a Facebook page participants are invited to respond to the prompt "relationship status." The normal responses are single, married, divorced, etc. However, once in a while someone responds: *it's complicated.* That leads me to believe that they are in a relationship but not *really* in a relationship—that is complicated.

The same can be true when it comes to healing from childhood emotional wounds: it's complicated. The mere passing of time doesn't make us whole. Simply saying the words "I'm over that" doesn't make it so, nor does burying the pain deep in the recesses of our mind. Healing is a process and if most of us are honest we know that getting over our past is—well—complicated.

As a child I was sensitive; every harsh word and disapproving look wounded me. Because of my sensitive nature I quickly adopted the belief that I wasn't good enough. That false belief, which shaped my worldview for many years, became the foundation for my identity and produced fruit. This is how that belief influenced my thought life and behavior:

THE FALSE BELIEF:

I AM NOT GOOD ENOUGH.

THE FRUIT OF THAT BELIEF:

1. A poor self image that led to the following beliefs:
   a. If my peers accept me (especially the popular ones) that makes me good.
   b. If I associate with those who *others* perceive as good I, by association, will be good too.
   c. If I am pleasing to those who are in authority, they will like me and infer goodness upon me.
2. A propensity for perfectionism:
   a. If I become perfect in every way (i.e., style of dress, talk, education, hair, makeup, etc.) no one will ever learn my secret shame—that I am not good enough.

If you can't follow that it's okay because *it's complicated*; lies always are.

There are some of you who are fighting with God. He is telling you to fast from a certain belief or behavior that you believe you are "over" and you are refusing to re-visit that old issue. Well if God is leading you to do so, He knows that there is some rotten fruit that still needs picking.

Today, I know I am good enough but the fruit of pleasing (especially authority) still lingers (see blog post *Bold and Courageous*). But I declare at the end of these 40 days that fruit will be no more. God finds me pleasing and that is all that matters.

The scripture tells us that we must bring every thought into captivity to the obedience of Christ (see 2 Corinthians 10:5). The only way to challenge every rebellious thought is to study and meditate on God's word; let His truth become your truth.

Here's His truth. You don't need anyone to approve of or accept you because God loves you just the way you are (see I John 4:19). If you meditate on His word day and night, do all that it says, you will make your way prosperous and have good success (see Joshua 1:8).

Now that's the truth and the truth is never complicated.

Personal Reflections

1. *How is the Spirit speaking to you?* Reflect on 2 Corinthians 10:5 and I John 4:19 and journal your insights.

2. What lies, if any, from childhood have you accepted as truth? In what ways do they continue to influence your thoughts and behavior?

3. Do these lies also affect your current relationships? If yes, with whom and in what way?

4. How would you like for God to change you over the next 40 days?

Day 1

Expect the Unexpected

"'For My thoughts are not your thoughts,
Nor are your ways My ways,' says the LORD.
'For as the heavens are higher than the earth,
So are My ways higher than your ways,
And My thoughts than your thoughts.'"

(Isaiah 55:8-9)

Welcome to Day 1 of the Surrender Fast! If your life is anything like mine, God has already started working on your heart and making it ready to receive more of Him.

We are a diverse group: men and women, young and seasoned, from Buffalo to Oakland. What we're surrendering is also quite varied. Some are fasting from food, some from lack of trust; while others relinquish fear, selfishness, pride, and insecurity. Each journey will be different, but we are all united in a single cause: to draw closer to God. I encourage you to keep notes and journal your experience.

As you have learned from reading the Pre-Fast Preparation posts, I am surrendering timidity to God. I will no longer be fearful but bold and courageous. For the next 40 days I will actively listen to the Holy Spirit's direction and step out boldly as He leads.

So God's first assignment—read about humility. That wasn't quite the direction I was expecting but I know from my other two fasts to expect the unexpected. The scripture tells us that God's ways are not our ways, nor His thoughts our thoughts.

So in obedience I am reading "Humility" by Andrew Murray. He says that humility is the place of total dependence on God. He further writes:

> Humility is not a thing we bring to God. It is also not a thing God gives to us. It is simply the realization of what nothings we really are, when we truly see how God is Everything, and when we clear out room in our hearts so that He can be everything for us.

I certainly want God to be my everything. Therefore, each morning I will commit my time to God: I will pray, read His word, and meditate on what I have read. You must make the same commitment. Growth won't occur by osmosis; a dream comes with much business and painful effort (see Ecclesiastes 4:3). If you want to experience a new thing in God, you must do your part. Hence, humble yourself before the King of Glory, listen to His instructions, and move as He directs. Freedom is on the way.

Personal Reflections

1. How is the Spirit speaking to you? Reflect on Psalm 25:9, 69:32, 147:6; James 4:10; and I Peter 5:6 and journal your insights.

2. From the start God is instructing us to be humble. What does humility mean to you? How is it related to the act of surrender?

3. Sometimes people are afraid to display humility because they associate meekness with weakness. Is there a difference between humility and being a pushover? How would you explain the difference?

4. On a scale from one to ten, what is your commitment level to reading God's word daily, reading this devotional and praying? Explain your ranking.

Day 2

Time, Effort, Reward

"Sow for yourselves righteousness;
Reap in mercy;
Break up your fallow ground,
For it is time to seek the LORD,
Till He comes and rains righteousness on you."

(Hosea 10:12)

It is said that time plus effort equals reward. This philosophy is true for most everything in life, present fast included. God has promised you a "new thing" and that promise most likely prompted you to join this fast. Therefore, be assured that He sees your sacrifice and will reward you according to your investment. In other words, over the next 38 days the time that you spend investing in your relationship with God will pay off handsomely.

The scripture tells us that what a man sows, he reaps (see Galatians 6:7). We are also reminded that if you sow sparingly, you will reap sparingly and if you sow bountifully, you will reap bountifully (see II Corinthians 9:6). Like you, I am expecting a mighty move of God during the course of this fast so I am sowing generously, but sowing requires a sacrifice. Therefore, I am making my comfort of little importance. I am neglecting that extra hour of sleep and cutting out activities that hinder my ability to seek God with all my heart. What about you? Are you investing in what matters? I know it's only day 2 but a strong finish requires a strong start.

For that reason, surrender your maladaptive habits to the Lord. Allow Him to break up the fallow, unfruitful ground in your heart and seed it with His plans and purposes. Seek Him with all that is in you, and require His favor until He comes and rains righteousness upon you.

The new thing you seek is here but your possession of it requires time and effort. Thus, rise early in the morning to give Him praise and seek His direction through prayer and the reading of His word. This little investment of your time will reap an abundant reward.

Personal Reflections

1. How is the Spirit speaking to you? Reflect on Hosea 10:12; Galatians 6:7; and II Corinthians 9:6 and journal your insights.

2. What sacrifices will you make in order to draw closer to God?

3. Typically what is your commitment level when it comes to starting new regiments? Are you readily committed to a plan from the beginning and follow it through to the end? Or are you commitment phobic? If the latter, what do you fear about commitment?

4. If you have identified fears, discuss them with your accountability partner. Pray and ask God to strengthen you so that you are able to push through the fear and succeed to the finish. If you are naturally a committed person, thank God for this gift and ask Him how He would like to use you to help develop this character trait in others.

Day 3

Rebuild and Renew

"And they shall rebuild the old ruins,
They shall raise up the former desolations,
And they shall repair the ruined cities,
The desolations of many generations."

(Isaiah 61:4)

Yesterday's blog revealed a basic truth: an investment of time and effort reaps a reward. What a marvelous reason to rejoice. Surrendering certainly has its benefits. In another 37 days we will have the benefit of a more intimate relationship with God, improved emotional health, and breakthroughs in many other areas of our lives.

Yet God has revealed another benefit. Let me invite you to think outside the box; beyond your short-sided view of reality. This fast has benefits that extend way beyond you. Ephesians 3:20 reads, "Now to Him who is able to do exceedingly abundantly above all that we ask or think, according to the power that works in us."

How many of you have been praying for your families and praying for God's favor and the miracle that only He can perform? The time is now; the shift is occurring. You can't see it in the natural but in the spiritual change is here.

That brother you have been praying for, God is doing in Him what He has promised. That child who has strayed, God is bringing her back. Those generational curses—debt, depression, molestation, anger, broken marriages, abandonment—God is making new.

Your radical act of faith is doing the impossible. Your surrender delights God. The scripture reminds us to, "Delight yourself also in the LORD, And He shall give you the desires of your heart" (Psalm 37:4).

God is now excited about acting on your behalf. Because of YOU He is repairing the ancient cities and the devastation of many generations; he is restoring the breaches. What a marvelous thing He is doing. Rejoice for it is already done!

Think about it. What abundant thing will God do for you and your family as a result of this fast? What generational curses will He break? I am the oldest of eight. Seven of us have accepted Christ as our personal savior. I declare, in Jesus' name that He will save my brother Stephen within the 38 days that we have left. We (me and my three sisters who are also on this fast) are rejoicing for it is already done.

Personal Reflections

1. How is the Spirit speaking to you? Reflect on Isaiah 61 and journal your insights.

2. Dr. Celeste mentioned some of the benefits of surrendering: more intimate relationship with God, improved emotional health, and breakthroughs in many other areas of your life. Can you think of any other benefits?

3. What impossible thing has God done for you in the past? What was that and how did it increase your faith?

4. What abundant thing will God do for you and your family as a result of this fast? What generational curses are you asking Him to break? Do you believe that He can and will do it?

Day 4

The Other Side

"On the same day, when evening had come,
He said to them,
'Let us cross over to the other side.'"

(Mark 4:35)

I'll let you in on a little secret…blogging is not my comfort zone, neither is writing for that matter. I do them both in obedience to God. That first Monday I blogged, I was amazed at what God wrote through me and excited for what He was to do for His people. However, the overwhelming response to the post sent me into a near panic as I thought, *"I can't do that again; I can't deliver another piece that will speak to the hearts of so many."* But as I let the Holy Spirit speak to my emotional storm, His peace enveloped me and calmed my fears.

The disciples experienced a similar panic in Mark chapter 4. One evening, after a long day of ministering, Jesus announced that they would cross to the other side. No doubt this was an exciting moment. *What new adventures would they experience on the other side?* Well, no sooner had they begun their journey, they experienced a storm.

Needless to say, the disciples hadn't anticipated such an occurrence. This storm was of monstrous proportion and they panicked. But what they did next is what we all are to do in the midst of a storm—they cried out to Jesus. In an instant He made the winds and sea behave and brought an immediate calm.

Likewise, Jesus has said to each of you, "Let's cross to the other side." In other words, "Let me do a new thing." No doubt your excitement is great: *what might this other side bring?* Don't be surprised when it's a storm.

Each morning before each post and in the midst of my emotional storm, I remind myself that I am doing His work not mine. Armed with that truth, I take a deep breath, whisper a prayer, read my word, and write. The peace that envelopes me during this process calms my fear and allows me to have an experience with God like no other.

Let His peace rest on you as well. For the next 36 days, remember that you are not making these sacrifices in your own strength. Whatever He has asked you to release to Him is His will and you will succeed. "Eye has not seen, nor ear heard, nor have entered into the heart of man the things which God has prepared for those who love Him" (I Corinthians 2:9). Be blessed.

Personal Reflections

1. How is the Spirit speaking to you? Reflect on Mark 4:35-41 and journal your insights.

2. What storms have begun in your life as a result of your surrender?

3. What can the disciples teach you about enduring the storm?

4. Like Dr. Celeste, is God requiring you to step out of your comfort zone; to do some activities that you are fearful of doing? How long have you avoided this activity? Will you finally heed His voice?

Day 5

It Will Come to Pass

*"Every word of God is pure;
He is a shield to those who put their trust in Him."*

(Proverbs 30:5)

It may not look like it right now, but every promise that God has made to you will come to pass. If you abide in Him, He will protect you and the dream He planted in your heart so long ago.

It's easy to become discouraged and discontent from today's vantage point. But our "now" doesn't necessarily reflect our tomorrow. The scripture reads, "It has not yet been revealed what we shall be" (I John 3:2a). I don't know about you, but in a year's time, I won't be what I am today. Better yet, in 35 days, I won't be what I am today. Each day I am improving and growing in Him.

Over the years, many a godly word has been spoken over me. It has been said that I will have the "ministry of marriage" and that I will be speaking to thousands. None of that is evident right now. Andel and I have a great marriage, but we aren't ministering to couples. I speak publicly, but certainly not to thousands. Does that mean those things aren't coming to pass? Absolutely not!

It is written, if you are faithful over a few He will make you ruler over many (see Matthew 25:23). Likewise, the word encourages us to appreciate the day of small beginnings, for it is in this time of preparation that He makes us ready for the greater things of Him (see Zechariah 4:10).

Therefore, I am using each day to prepare for what is to come. Andel and I regularly fast for the welfare of couples, and I speak with zeal to every audience that comes under the sound of my voice. In God's timing, I will transcend to greater heights in Him; but it's what I do today—in excellence—that builds the firm foundation for what is to come.

Beloved, don't let today stifle your hopes for tomorrow. Keep the faith, God's word will not return to Him void. He promises that not one of all the good things He has spoken concerning you will fail and ALL will come to pass (see Joshua 21:45, 23:14).

Personal Reflections

1. How is the Spirit speaking to you? Reflect on Proverbs 30:5 and Joshua 21:45, 23:14 and journal your insights.

2. What promises have God spoken to you that have yet to come to pass? Do you believe that He will do just as He has said?

3. What preparations are you making for the manifestation of each promise?

4. Sometimes as we wait we become anxious for the manifestation of God's plan. Are you content with today or anxious for tomorrow? If the latter, what will you do to maintain balance as you wait?

Day 6

Personal Time with God

SCRIPTURE(S):

HOW IS THE SPIRIT SPEAKING TO YOU?

DAY 7

Personal Time with God

SCRIPTURE(S):

HOW IS THE SPIRIT SPEAKING TO YOU?

DAY 8

Establish Your Faith

*"And whatever you ask in My name, that I will do,
that the Father may be glorified in the Son.
If you ask anything in My name, I will do it."*

(John 14:13-14)

I am excited to report that my first big bold and courageous moment occurred this weekend as I ministered to the Cancer Support Ministry of the First Baptist Church of Glenarden. It was a powerful session.

My parents, in town for a short visit, attended the seminar and shared some words of encouragement to the group. One statement made by my mother struck a chord with me. She said that she would never get cancer. That is a bold statement considering that she has an extensive family history of various cancers and statistics conclude that she too will suffer with the disease. But she knows that God isn't moved by statistics and His plan will come to pass no matter her history. That's why when He had instructed her (at a prior speaking engagement) to declare that she would never get cancer, she did. And she has been saying it ever since.

I had never made such a declaration and didn't intend to do so that day, but as I stood before the people the words "I will never be stricken with cancer again in Jesus' name" came out of my mouth. I felt both a mix of excitement and power as I proclaimed what I knew to be true. And in that moment I established my faith.

Establishing or activating your faith is the process of doing in the natural what God has already finished in the spiritual. The scripture declares that faith without works is dead (James 2:20) and that without faith it is impossible to please the Lord (see Hebrews 11:6). Therefore, on that Saturday, I did what God had been urging me to do for months. Let me explain.

Just a few months prior to that event I had spoken at a cancer fundraising event. During the speech, I made the statement "I don't believe that I will get cancer again but if I do I will trust God for my healing." I felt a little strange making that statement and I didn't understand why, but now I do. We are told in Proverbs 18:21 that life and death are in the power of the tongue and in James 3:10 that the tongue can speak both blessings and curses. I now know that when I said the words, "I don't believe that I will...but if I do..." my doubt left room for the disease to attack me again.

For that reason, on Saturday, September 18, 2010 in Conference Room 2, before a group of cancer survivors, God challenged me to establish my faith; to say aloud the words my soul had longed to hear, *I will never be stricken with cancer again in Jesus' name.* Now if that isn't bold and courageous, I don't know what is!

Some of you are wondering: *how can she make such a claim? How can she say with certainty that she will never get cancer again?* I can do so because God's word gives me permission. Jesus said that I can ask anything in His name and He will do it. Furthermore, when I am living a life surrendered unto Him, I am able to accurately discern His will and know what to ask for.

My friends, faith is more than mere words; it is an attitude of confidence that knows without a shadow of doubt that God will do just as He has promised. I implore you today, and for the next 32 days, to establish your faith with boldness and watch His will come to pass. Be blessed in Jesus' name.

Personal Reflections

1. How is the Spirit speaking to you? Reflect on John 14:12-14 and journal your insights.

2. Establishing or activating your faith is only possible when you believe the God will do just what He has said. How convinced are you that God will work things out for your good? In which areas of your life do you need to trust God more?

3. The scripture tells us that faith without works is dead (see James 2:26). What does that mean to you? In which areas of your life do you need to establish your faith?

4. There is power in sharing with another trusted individual what you believe God will do for you. Tell your accountability partner what you are expecting God to do.

Day 9

Pray for Your Enemies

"Do not rejoice when your enemy falls,
And do not let your heart be glad when he stumbles;
Lest the LORD see it, and it displease Him,
And He turn away His wrath from him."

(Proverbs 24:17-18)

If you have lived any amount of time someone has wronged you. Some offenses have been slight while others major. Nonetheless, the Bible gives clear instructions on how to handle these offenses. It states, "Love your enemies, bless those who curse you, do good to those who hate you, and pray for those who spitefully use you and persecute you," (Matthew 5:44).

It's human nature to wish bad on someone who has hurt you, to seek revenge, and/or shut down emotionally. However, a mature Christian, one that has matured in love, accesses the power surging within him to respond in a way that defies his nature. The scriptures reads, "I can do all things through Christ that strengthens me" (Philippians 4:13). That includes forgiving those who spitefully use you.

It's easy to love those who love you, but the proof of your conversion is reflected in your ability to love those who use you, who take advantage of your kindness, and wish harm upon you.

Christ experienced similar maltreatment. During His public ministry He was rejected, talked about, abandoned and crucified—not only by those who hated Him, but also His closest confidants. Judas betrayed Him, Peter denied Him, and Thomas needed proof of his resurrection.

Yet in the face of unfathomable rejection, Christ died for us all. And even today, despite continual rejection, He persists in heaping blessings upon His brothers and sisters. Despite our wrongdoings, He sits at the right hand of God praying for us and pleading to God on our behalf. Therefore, let Christ be your perfect example. Because He has forgiven you of so much and continues to seek your good, return the favor to some wayward soul.

During this time of surrender, allow the Spirit to speak to you about the condition of your heart. What attitudes and beliefs does He need to rid you of in the next 31 days? The time is now; God is doing a new thing, but unforgiveness and other revenge-seeking behaviors will hinder your forward movement.

Therefore, choose the higher road—the path of love. Allow God to heal you of your hurt so that He can use you in a supernatural way in the lives of others. May God's favor be upon you today and forevermore.

Personal Reflections

1. How is the Spirit speaking to you? Reflect on Proverbs 24:17-18 and journal your insights.

2. Pray and ask God to reveal to you the condition of your heart. A prayer that I often whisper is, "God show me, me." Is He revealing to you a person or persons that you have not forgiven? If yes, what will you do to make this right?

3. Forgiveness for those who have hurt us goes against our nature. Why then does God require us to forgive? What are the benefits of forgiving? What are the consequences of unforgiveness? Find scriptures to validate your answers.

4. What does Christ's sacrifice mean to you and how does it demonstrate how you are to love?

Day 10

Renewal is Necessary

"And He said to them,
'Come aside by yourselves to a deserted place
and rest a while.'
For there were many coming and going, and
they did not even have time to eat."

(Mark 6:31)

We live in a society where everyone wants to appear busy. This seems to be especially true of the DMV (the District, Maryland, and Virginia). In the last year, I have rejected the notion of busy; outright refusing to use the "b" word. Whenever someone says to me, "I know you are busy but…," I quickly correct their perception of my life informing them that I am not busy, but productive.

Some may consider this a simple matter of semantics, but to the contrary. Busy and productive are two different concepts and states of being. I have learned that "busy" is about me, while "productive" is about God.

When I am busy for the sake of being busy, I am scattered, drained, frustrated, and inefficient. When I am productive in the things of God, I am focused, content, joyful and at peace.

That's exactly what God wants for us all. He wants us to live in the peace that surpasses all understanding, to have unspeakable joy, and to prosper in all things. If you find yourself continuously frustrated, you need to recalibrate your life and some good old-fashioned rest may be the best place to start.

You may not want to rest but it is necessary. We aren't always to be "on." Jesus understood that very well. For that reason in Mark 6, Jesus instructed His disciples to take a break from labor. He knew that in their rest they would find renewal and the strength to be productive in the next leg of their race.

So why then do we reject rest? Pride. In fact, all busy behavior is driven by pride. Your pride drives you to believe that you can't stop, you are indispensable, and that others can't make it without you. But that is a trick of the enemy to keep you busy and unproductive. Trust me, if you died today, your friends and family would find a way to make it without you.

Therefore, I implore you to surrender you time to God and be wholly dependent on Him. Likewise, make sure the next 30 days are productive and about Him. It is in His presence that you will find the fullness of joy and rest for your soul.

Personal Reflections

1. How is the Spirit speaking to you? Reflect on Mark 6:30-32 and journal your insights.

2. Based on Dr. Celeste's definition, are you primarily busy or primarily productive? If you are prone to busyness what do you say drives your behavior and motivates you to keep up a pattern of busyness? If, however, you are mostly productive what safeguards have you put in place to maintain this balanced lifestyle?

3. When you are busy for the sake of being busy, how is pride driving your behavior?

4. Are you getting enough rest? If not, what will you do to make this a regular part of your daily renewal?

5. What activities or circumstances is the Holy Spirit urging you to eliminate? Are there certain relationships you need to sever? Will you obey His leading? Why or why not?

Day 11

Peculiar Am I

"But ye are a chosen generation, a royal priesthood,
an holy nation, a peculiar people;
that ye should shew forth the praises of
him who hath called you out of darkness
into his marvelous light."

(I Peter 2:9, KJV)

I'm different; I always have been. In grade school my parents joined the Pentecostal church which had certain rules. One rule was that women couldn't wear pants. So I wore skirts from kindergarten on into high school. In Buffalo, New York, a city known for its terrible winters, my behavior was odd.

In college, I desperately wanted to fit in; to be "normal." Because most of my friends cursed I thought I would try, but when I did they asked me to stop. One friend even declared that I was hurting his ears. What a pity, I couldn't even curse properly.

I'm not a big medicine person because we were taught in the Pentecostal church to pray to God for our healing. The first time our son was sick, I prayed for his healing and went about my business. A few hours later my husband asked, "What did you give him for the fever?" I replied, "I prayed." Boy, did I look strange.

I've always been told that I run funny. One day my three-year-old daughter Aaliyah challenged me to a race to the mailbox. We took off. Aaliyah, graceful and elegant, looked like a sprinter. I, in my flat-footed, pigeon-toed style of jog, looked, well, different. As we ran I heard a car approaching, I could feel them saying, "she runs funny." So what else is new? I'm different...and I'm willing to bet you are too.

But that's okay because different is good and being different puts us in great company. Jesus, the greatest person to ever grace this earth was also different. He was born of a virgin, lived on the wrong side of the tracks (someone was even heard saying, "Can any good thing come from Nazareth?"), lacked formal education, ate with sinners, healed on the Sabbath, and died to give us life. Now if that's not different, I don't know what is. However, if He embraced His unique identity, so can we! We are a royal priesthood, a peculiar people set aside to do something great in God.

God is preparing you for your next phase in Him, but you must first accept the "you" that He has called you to be. It doesn't matter what others have said or think about you, as long as you are pleasing to God that is all that matters. Remember He loves you and me—peculiarities and all— just the way we are.

Personal Reflections

1. How is the Spirit speaking to you? Reflect on I Peter 2:4-10 and journal your insights.

2. Can you relate to Dr. Celeste's sentiment about being different? If so, in what ways are you different? Are you okay with that?

3. What personality or character traits do you find most challenging to accept?

4. In what way might being different positively influence your ability to fulfill the call that God has on your life?

5. We have the power to speak life. Identify at least one person you can encourage that is struggling with being different? What will you say to encourage him/her? What portion of your testimony could you share that would help them embrace their uniqueness?

Day 12

God's Friend

"I love those who love me,
And those who seek me diligently will find me."

(Proverbs 8:17)

Yesterday I had a major decision to make. Should I, or should I not continue to write for a particular magazine. I prayed about it and sensed God's answer, but still needed confirmation, so I phoned my prayer partner. We talked, and at the end of a very brief conversation she stated, "You had the answer all along."

How true were her words; *I had the answer all along.* I had prayed, God had answered yet I was doubtful.

Perhaps some of you have had a similar experience; doubting that you had heard from God when indeed you had. Or maybe you are in the habit of seeking advice from others without first seeking God's face. Whatever the case, Proverbs 8:17 offers some insight. Let's dissect it:

I love those who love me.

The word "love" here comes from the Hebrew word *ahab* which means to love like a friend or ally. Of course we know of God's agape (unconditional) love, but for Him to love us as friend is an added benefit.

Take a moment to think about your earthly friendships. What essential qualities characterize a good friendship? Is it quality time, uncensored conversation, and/or confidence that that person has your back? Well the same should be true of your friendship with God. He doesn't just want to be your bail-out plan or the one you call when all other hope is lost. No, He desires to be your friend and connected with you in a meaningful way.

Those who seek me early and diligently shall find me.

A meaningful relationship with God includes seeking His advice first, not just when you are in trouble. Wouldn't it be aggravating to have a friend who only came to you when he/she was in need? At some point you might consider distancing yourself from him/her. But how many times have we turned to God at the end of a matter, when all (human) hope is gone? My friend, that should not be so. We should be in a posture of total dependence on Him, seeking Him early for every situation. Not only early in the morning but at the beginning of the drama!

Therefore, make God your priority; seek His face, desire His presence, and become His friend. His word promises, "Then you shall call, and the Lord will answer; you shall cry, and He will say, Here I am" (Isaiah 58:9a).

What an awesome promise from our friend! He hears our prayer and will answer—and from now on I will trust His reply.

Personal Reflections

1. How is the Spirit speaking to you? Reflect on Proverbs 8:17 and journal your insights.

2. What is your first reaction when you have a dilemma? Do you first discuss it with family and friends then go to God or do you go to God first?

3. God speaks to us differently, but He can often be heard as a still small voice speaking to our spirits. Have you learned to hear God's voice for yourself?

4. How do you know when He is speaking to you? Besides a still small voice, in what other ways could He speak to you?

5. Do you consider yourself God's friend? What steps will you take to draw even closer to Him?

Day 13

Personal Time with God

Scripture(s):

How is the Spirit speaking to you?

Day 14

Personal Time with God

SCRIPTURE(S):

HOW IS THE SPIRIT SPEAKING TO YOU?

Day 15

I Declare War!

"For we do not wrestle against flesh and blood, but
against principalities,
against powers, against the rulers of the darkness of this age,
against spiritual hosts of wickedness in the heavenly places."

(Ephesians 6:12, KJV)

As I rose from my knees this morning, the Holy Spirit directed me to write on spiritual warfare. Little did I know that I would have to experience it before I could post to this blog!

Of all the things that could happen while blogging, losing the internet connection is probably one of the worst. Well that's just what happened. I spent over an hour booting, rebooting, checking cords, and clicking buttons with no success.

I wanted to give in to the frustration, but I willed my emotions to do the opposite of my nature. So with a calm exterior I proceeded with my morning routine: dressing the children, dropping them off to school—all the while praying that God would rebuke the enemy from this situation. Thankfully, He did and I was finally able to post this blog.

What was that all about you ask? It's about the enemy being displeased with what God is doing; about him trying to frustrate a situation so that I will give up. But it will take a lot more than that for me to give up on God's plan for you and me.

You may be experiencing similar frustrations. Take a moment to think about what you have surrendered to God. Has the journey been easy or challenging? I would suspect that these past two weeks have been quite taxing.

Perhaps you've surrendered fear to God, yet every fear-producing situation that can happen has; maybe you're watching your words, but people and circumstances are exasperating you beyond belief; or perhaps you've committed your mornings to God only to have your alarm clock not go off. I could go on, but I think you get the picture: *there's a fight going on and we are in the middle.*

Don't be surprised when everything that could go wrong, does. The enemy, in his frustration with you, has declared all out war, but be encouraged. The scripture reminds us that, "Greater is He that is in me than He that is in the world (I John 4:4)." Accordingly, you have authority over the enemy and he has to conform to your commands.

The military has a code they use when they're on high alert. It's code red. For the next 25 days we are on high alert. Sound the alarm, there is a war going on, but with God on our side we will win!

These are the tools that you need to combat all that the enemy is sending your way:

1. *The Word* – meditate on it day and night. Commit to memory the scripture(s) that speak to your situation.
2. *Prayer* – active communication with God will strengthen your relationship with Him and allow you to feel His grace as He carries you through these challenging circumstances.

3. *Spiritual Support* – one form of spiritual support comes from this blog. But other sources of support could come from your spouse, family members, friends, and/or prayer partner(s).

4. *Self-control* – the enemy isn't interested in your comfort. He will continue to mess with you though you are frustrated, angry and/or tearful. No matter what, WILL your mind to come under subjection to the Holy Spirit. Be a good soldier and endure until the end.

Don't take Satan's tactics lying down; get on your knees and exercise the authority that Christ has given you. Say with all power, "I rebuke you in the name of Jesus" and he will flee (see James 4:7).

God placed a song in my heart this morning by Wes Morgan. When I got into my car it was playing on the radio (don't you love how God does that?). The lyrics go, "He's healing me…I'm going to worship." Rejoice today, for every crooked place God is making straight; He is making a way in the wilderness and rivers in deserts.

Nonetheless, the enemy is displeased, so suit up. There is a war going on and with God we will win!

Personal Reflections

1. How is the Spirit speaking to you? Reflect on Ephesians 6:10-12 and journal your insights.

2. Spiritual warfare is real. The enemy is determined to discourage you from completing this fast. In what ways has he challenged your faith? What safeguards have you or will you put in place to secure your successful completion of this fast?

3. It always helps to recall past victories. Have there been other times that you felt like you were in a war or spiritual battle? What was the outcome? What did you do to stay strengthened?

4. What we believe is often evident in how we behave. Earlier Dr. Celeste mentioned how important it is to exhibit self-control, especially when it comes to controlling your emotions. How are you behaving during this fast? Are you grumbling and complaining or confident and positive?

5. Do you wholeheartedly believe that God has given you power over the enemy? If yes, do your thoughts and behavior reflect a heart of belief?

DAY 16

Superhuman

"But those who wait on the LORD
Shall renew their strength;
They shall mount up with wings like eagles,
They shall run and not be weary,
They shall walk and not faint."

(Isaiah 40:31)

The other day I was watching Stan Lee's *Superhumans* on the History Channel. The title is self-descriptive. Each episode features people who do amazing feats that defy nature. The particular show I watched featured a gentleman that could run and never tire. The show's scientist soon discovered why. Lactic acid, the chemical released in the body during strenuous exercise that leads to fatigue, remained at low levels in his body at all times. For this reason he was deemed a superhuman.

The strength this man exhibited in his natural body is akin to the strength that we, who are in Christ, can access in the spirit. In God we are super humans. His word confirms this truth. The prophet Isaiah wrote we shall run and not grow weary, walk and not faint.

One way this superhuman strength is acquired is through the process of waiting. "*What?! You might ask.*

Simply waiting?" Trust me, there is nothing simple about waiting; it defies our nature. The flesh wants everything right now, this instant. However, it is said that anything worth having, is worth waiting for, and God's blessings are certainly worth the wait.

I remember the day that I was accepted to the University of Pittsburgh for their doctorate program. I was super excited. The phone call from the faculty member started well, but soon took a sour turn when he shared with me that the program didn't have the funds to allow me to attend for free (which had been one of my stipulations). I was disappointed but unwilling to compromise because God had told me that He would fully fund this leg of my education. So I boldly told him that I would have to decline admittance unless they found me funding. Then I waited.

The wait wasn't easy. Several times I was tempted to call them back and accept the offer without funding. But each time I felt that way, I prayed, and God renewed my strength. Three weeks later I received the phone call I had been waiting for. They had found enough money to fund my entire doctorate degree! Because I trusted in God's promises and waited, I was rewarded.

Stop trying to make things happen in your own strength. If God said it, He will do it. Isaiah 55:11 reads, "So shall My word be that goes forth from My mouth; It shall not return to Me void, But it shall accomplish what I please, And it shall prosper *in the thing* for which I sent it."

If you are waiting on God for a promotion...wait; a husband...wait; a new job...wait; acceptance into a program...wait. Although everything around you may be falling apart and things aren't going the way you planned, He is in control and will work it out in due time.

Therefore I declare that you, too, can be super human if you simply wait on God and let His supernatural power work in your life.

Personal Reflections

1. How is the Spirit speaking to you? Reflect on Isaiah 40:26-31 and journal your insights.

2. How are you at waiting? Do you want everything right now or have you learned to wait on God? In what ways can you improve your attitude during your wait time?

3. What are you waiting for the Lord to do in your life? How long have you been waiting? What is most challenging about the wait? Do you trust God to do for you what He said He will do?

4. Like Dr. Celeste, have you ever received news about a situation that was contrary to the word that God had given you? What did you do? Did you compromise or did you wait? What was the outcome?

DAY 17

The God in Me

"The ark of the LORD remained in the house of
Obed-Edom the Gittite three months.
And the LORD blessed Obed-Edom and all his household."

(II Samuel 6:11)

H ave you ever wondered why you are where you are? Why God has placed you at a certain job, church, community group, school, or even family? I certainly have.

I remember once working a job that I hated. I was miserable and made sure that God (and even those I worked with) knew it. I prayed that He would move me but my prayers seemed to fall on deaf ears. What I didn't understand then, was that God had a plan. He needed me there and He wasn't going to move me until His plans had been fulfilled.

Since that time I have learned to recognize God's sovereign hand in all of my situations. A story that reminds me of the importance of doing that is told in II Samuel 6. As the story goes, David and the children of Israel had been in the process of transporting the ark of God to the city of Jerusalem, when tragedy stuck. One of their own, Uzzah, was killed by God when he touched the ark. David, deeply trouble by this occurrence, aborted the transporting mission. He then left the ark in the home of Obed-Edom, the brother of the deceased.

I can only imagine Obed-Edom's "delight" to have the ark that had killed his brother, reside in his home. He may have wondered if he would face the same fate or he may have longed to be free from the obligation of housing the ark. However, God wasn't moving the ark until He was ready. What Obed-Edom failed to realize was that God's presence always brings blessings. For the three months that the ark remained with Obed-Edom, he and his entire household were blessed.

This story has huge implications for how we are to approach life today. Just like Obed-Edom, we will be called to seasons we don't want to weather or like the ark be placed in situations where we are unwanted. There will also be times when we will be despised and rejected because of the God in us. Nonetheless, if we keep the faith and trust in God's plan, those around us will be blessed. Not because we are so good, but because God's presence resides in us. His word reads, "where the Spirit of the Lord *is,* there *is* liberty" (2 Corinthians 3:17, NKJV). Therefore, those in direct contact with us should feel His presence and find rest.

In light of this truth, stop fighting God's plan and complaining about your station in life. You may not understand it all now, but He does, so trust that He has a plan and that it will work out for your good. If you are willing to endure a little discomfort for a season, others will have the awesome opportunity to see God in you and be blessed beyond measure.

Personal Reflections

1. How is the Spirit speaking to you? Reflect on II Samuel 6:11 and journal your insights.

2. Have you been or are you now in a place where you would rather not be? Explain your situation.

3. If you are in a challenging situation now, are you representing God well?

4. Are others being blessed because you are in their presence? Are they able to see the love of God radiating from you? If not, what will you do to be a better representation of God?

DAY 18

The Keys for Good Relationships

"Behold, how good and how pleasant it is
For brethren to dwell together in unity!"

(Psalm 133:1)

Unless you live on a deserted island, you are in relationship with at least one other person. For some this is easy—he/she finds freedom in being in relationship with others—while for others, relationships are challenging to say the least.

God emphasizes numerous times in scripture the importance of being in unity with others. He knows that healthy vibrant living is contingent upon the quality of our relationships. Research indicates this is especially true of women; love is everything in the life of a woman. For her, the lack of healthy, thriving relationships can lead to depression, anxiety and other psychological problems. This fact of life confirms that God designed us to be in healthy relationships and to dwell in unity. Let's discuss two ways to maintain unity:

1. ***Resolve conflicts without involving a third party (when possible).*** I believe that most conflicts in relationships can be resolved by going directly to the person with whom you are in conflict. The Bible confirms that this is the best first step for resolving conflict. Matthew 18:15a reads, "Moreover if your brother sins against you, go and tell him his fault between you and him alone."

a. How many times have you been in conflict with someone and instead of going to the source of your conflict you involve another person (who usually has nothing to do with the problem or the solution). In the field of psychology this is called triangulation. For example, a husband and wife who are having problems "triangle" in their child; two co-workers are communicating ineffectively so one or both "triangle" in a third co-worker. This technique may relieve anxiety for the short-term, but it is a cowardly way to resolve conflicts.

b. True resolution requires a quieting of your fears (e.g., If I confront the person they won't like me anymore, or if I confront them they will think ill of me.). Fear is a powerful de-motivator so if you are to succeed at relationships and dwell in unity, fear can't be a part of your resolution process.

2. ***Forsake the need to be right all the time.*** Do I need to say more? You aren't always right. It is human

nature to put ourselves in the best light however, the need to be right all of the time is a sign of insecurity.

I encourage you to entertain the thought that someone else might know something that you don't. I know it is sounds far-fetched, but try it on for size. You just might buy yourself some unity and some additional friendships. No one likes a know-it-all, but everyone is drawn to vulnerability and a teachable spirit.

Lastly, make up your mind today to dwell in unity in all your relationships; it will serve you well. If you have relationship in need of repair, ask the Holy Spirit to give you the words to speak so that the conflict is resolved. If your efforts don't work and you believe that the relationship is worth saving, find a "neutral" third party to help the two of you resolve your conflict. It will be worth the effort because obeying God's word in this matter will allow you to reap the benefits (e.g., peace, joy, etc.) of dwelling in peace-filled, unified relationships.

Personal Reflections

1. How is the Spirit speaking to you? Reflect on Psalm 133 and journal your insights.

2. How would you rate the quality of your relationships? Are they healthy and thriving or challenging and conflict-filled? What can you do to improve your relationships?

3. Is one or more of your relationships strained? What caused the strain and how did you play a part in all of this? What will you do to make it right?

4. Ultimately the quality of our relationships is a reflection of the relationship we have with God. What is your relationship like with God? Are you making time to seek Him?

5. If you don't love yourself, loving someone else is nearly impossible. How do you feel about you? Are there some unresolved issues that you need to address? Where will you start? Speak with your accountability partner about what the spirit is revealing to you about yourself.

Day 19

I Still Surrender

*"And they overcame him by the blood of the Lamb and
by the word of their testimony."*

(Revelation 12:11a)

We are nearly 50% of the way there. How are you faring? My experience with this fast gives me insight to where you might be in the process. Right about now, if you have committed your all to this fast, the surrender may seem as if it will overwhelm you. For example, if you surrendered "fear", you may feel consumed by it; if "control", everything may be falling apart; or if "spending more time with your children", every distraction that can come has.

To make matters worse, the enemy is probably bombarding you with every negative thought and circumstance he can drum up to get you to give up or start over—but don't. Persist through the pressure; you are nearly to the finish line. I assure you that somewhere around Day 28, or soon thereafter, you will start to feel a release. So hold on.

Tomorrow, I will have my next big bold and courageous moment. I am speaking to a group of 9th-12th grade girls at a women's conference with over 4,000 participants. "What's so challenging about that?" you might ask. Everything. Let me testify so that I can overcome by my words.

First, I am self-conscious around large groups of women. Secondly, God has instructed me to attend the conference without wearing makeup (specifically foundation). You would have to know my story to understand how women and makeup go together.

In a nutshell, as a teen I wasn't accepted by the girls that I thought mattered. As a result, I concluded that there was something wrong with me. I was just too different: I didn't talk or think like the other girls, I wore skirts all the time, and I had acne. Therefore, as an adult I worked really hard on projecting the perfect image. So began my love affair with makeup.

Oh yes, it has been a love affair. In fact, God told me it was an idol. Accordingly, He suggested in June of 2010 that I present at the Regional Lady of Virtue Conference in Buffalo, New York, without it. I fought God on His suggestion but He knew, as well as I, that He would win, because I love and trust Him, and (nearly) always comply with His requests.

Since that conference I haven't gone back to wearing the foundation. Not that it's wrong, just wrong for me right now. So when they announced that I would be one of the speakers at the First Baptist Church of Glenarden Women's Conference, I panicked. Me and 4,000 strange women who could reject me? No way. *I would definitely need to order some foundation*, I thought. Instantly the Holy Spirit forbade it. We literally argued back in forth, but with tears streaming down my face I decided to comply. I would not wear foundation to the conference.

That might seem small to you but for me it's major, bold and courageous, and crazy. But I am okay with that because at the end of this fast it will be worth it. I will obtain the ultimate prize: *freedom from every thought and pattern of living that keeps me from living a victorious life.* Now, that my friend, is well worth fighting for.

Your surrender is equally as important. You will be the victor if you faint not. You are almost to the finish line; be sure to see it through to the end.

Personal Reflections

1. How is the Spirit speaking to you? Reflect on Revelation 12:11a and journal your insights.

2. Have you been tempted to give up on this fast? How do you think your continued surrender will benefit you in the long run?

3. We all have had struggles. What childhood challenges influence the way you operate as an adult.

4. Sometimes it's embarrassing to share with another person what we are struggling with, but the scripture tells us that we overcome by the words of our testimony. Share with your accountability partner or other close friend one of your current challenges. How difficult will that be? How do you think it will help you?

Day 20

Personal Time with God

SCRIPTURE(S):

HOW IS THE SPIRIT SPEAKING TO YOU?

Day 21

Personal Time with God

SCRIPTURE(S):

HOW IS THE SPIRIT SPEAKING TO YOU?

Day 22

Dust off Your Dreams

*"For a dream comes through much activity,
And a fool's voice is known by his many words."*

(Ecclesiastes 5:3)

As mentioned in the previous post, I had the pleasure of ministering to 9th-12th grade girls at the First Baptist Church of Glenarden Women's Conference this past weekend. What a blessed time we had in the Lord! God's agenda was clear: *the girls are to dream big, dream bold, and always remember that He does not forget.* He reminded them that when He plants a dream in the heart, it comes to pass. That truth is confirmed in Habakkuk 2: 2-3.

Then the LORD answered me and said:

"Write the vision
And make *it* plain on tablets,
That he may run who reads it.
For the vision *is* yet for an appointed time;
But at the end it will speak, and it will not lie.
Though it tarries, wait for it;

Because it will surely come,
It will not tarry.

In the 7th grade, God planted a dream in my heart during 4th period study hall. While browsing the microfiche in the library I happened upon an article about a little boy who was killed by his mother. The story deeply troubled my spirit and it was in that instant God revealed to me part of His plan for my life. I knew then that I would be a psychologist.

The journey towards that dream was difficult. I had to fight for college funding, endure prejudice, and live meagerly. Nonetheless, His plan for my life came to pass in 2002 when I obtained my doctorate degree. I am now a psychologist.

Over the years God has planted many more dreams in my heart. Some have come to pass while others tarry. Am I worried? Not a bit. They too will come to pass if I wait on the Lord.

What are the dreams that God has planted in you? Well now is the time to dust them off, put them back on your agenda, and pursue them as God leads you. Don't get overly concerned with the details. Les Brown, motivational speaker, says "the *how* is none of your business." Trust that God has it all handled and He will provide the means. All He needs from you is your willingness to comply with His every command.

Research indicates that those who write down their dreams are substantially more likely to pursue and achieve them, than those who do not. Therefore, I encourage you to write out each and every one of your dreams today. Then place them in a place where you can see them on the run or as you go about your daily activities. Let them be a constant reminder of what God has promised. It's never too late…though the vision tarries it's only for a while, He will do just as He said.

Let me give you a quick word of caution. Be sure the dreams that you are pursuing are God's and not yours. Our flesh can get in the way and encourage us to pursue a dream that is not a part of God's plan for our lives. If you are unsure, pray to God for wisdom. Then ask Him to confirm His truth to you either through His word and/or godly people. When the dream is confirmed, believe that it will come to pass no matter what life brings your way.

Lastly, though a dream comes with much business and painful effort, the pursuit of a godly dream is well worth the fight. Be encouraged my sisters and brothers. God is not through with you yet and His dreams will come to pass!

Personal Reflections

1. How is the Spirit speaking to you? Reflect on Ecclesiastes 5:3 and Habakkuk 2: 2-4 and journal your insights.

2. What are your dreams? Write them down here or on another piece of paper. Are you on the road to fulfilling them? If not, what is holding you back?

3. Review your list of dreams. Choose one dream and write out specific steps that you need to take to make this dream a reality.

   For example: *I want to be a Surgical Tech*

   Step 1:   Research the qualifications needed to be a surgical tech.

   Step 2:   Talk with a surgical tech to get their opinion about the field.

   Step 3:   Apply to schools.

   Do this for each one of your dreams. Write out the steps that you need to follow below.

4. For many different reasons, people fear telling others about their dreams. Don't let that be you. Pick one of the dreams you listed in Question 2. Tell your accountability partner or a close friend about that dream. How did it feel to tell someone else? How did they respond?

DAY 23

Your Breakthrough is Coming Through

"Then it happened, as he drew back his hand,
that his brother came out unexpectedly; and she said,
'How did you break through? This breach be upon you!'
Therefore his name was called Perez."

(Genesis 38:29)

There is a story in the bible that has fascinated me for years. It comes from a chapter in the book of Genesis. I hadn't read it in a while, but this morning God spoke to me "Genesis 38." Honestly I couldn't remember what Genesis 38 pertained, but when I opened my bible to this passage of scripture, I knew. This was the story of the breakthrough.

Genesis 38 features Judah, the son of Jacob and brother to Joseph. As the story goes, Judah and his other brothers were very jealous of Joseph because of the love Jacob had for his son. Their hatred of Joseph led them to plot a scheme to rid themselves of him. As a result, he was sold into slavery.

Soon after this occurrence, Judah left home and moved in with his friend Hirah at Adullam. There, Judah met a woman, took her as his wife, and she bore him 3 sons: Er, Onan, and Shelah. When his eldest son Er was of age he married Tamar. Unfortunately, Er was evil in the sight of the Lord and He killed him.

His death left Tamar a widow, but not really. According to their custom, Onan, the second son was to take Tamar as his wife and raise offspring for his brother. Onan , not "feeling" his fate, prevented conception. This displeased the Lord, so He killed him.

Poor Tamar. Two husbands dead and still no heir. But there was one last hope: Shelah. Accordingly, Judah instructed Tamar to remain a widow in her father's house until Shelah came of age. Unfortunately, Judah had decided in his heart, now considering Tamar a jinx, that she would never have this son and with that her fate was sealed...or so he thought. But he had underestimated Tamar. She wouldn't take this course of action lying down, she had a plan.

When Tamar learned that Judah was visiting Timnath to shear his sheep, she pretended to be a harlot. Judah took the bait, and subsequently impregnated her. Some months later when he learned of her pregnancy, he ordered that she be stoned. However, when Tamar proved to him that he was the father, he proclaimed to all that were listening, "She has been more righteous than I, because I did not give her to Shelah my son."

Wow, total vindication. But the story doesn't end there. Tamar's "power move" landed her in the genealogy hall of fame. The son she bore, ironically named Perez which means breakthrough, carried on the messianic line until the time of David, and ultimately to Jesus. Matthew 1:3a reads, "Judah begot Perez and Zerah by Tamar."

What an amazing turn of events. This woman, who had to pretend to be a harlot to get her father-in-law to do right by her, gives birth to a child who is a descendent for our Lord and Savior! What a comeback.

Like Tamar, we've all been hurt by other people or victim to situations that were out of our control. Yet her story demonstrates the importance of allowing God to work things out. We certainly don't have to take the enemy's tactics lying down. Discouragement, fear, doubt, and guilt are from him, but with the power of God working in us, we can do something about our dead situations and change the course of our lives.

You may have been discounted, but that doesn't have to be your fate. You are in and not out, the victor and not the conquered, the head and not the tail, above and not beneath (see Deuteronomy 28). In Jesus' name your breakthrough is coming through and destined to arrive within the next 17 days. Stay strong in your faith, trust God and watch him orchestrate a comeback that will give Him all the glory.

Personal Reflections

1. How is the Spirit speaking to you? Reflect on Genesis 38 and journal your insights.

2. Are you in need of a breakthrough? Do you believe that God can and will deliver you from whatever you are challenged by right now? What will you do to keep your faith strong?

3. Who has been your "Judah"? What did they do? In what way, if any, does this hurt still affect you today?

4. God doesn't waste pain. Tamar was rewarded handsomely for the hurt that she endured at the hand of Judah. Can you see how the hurts of your life have been or will be for God's greater plan? In not, pray and ask God to open the eyes of your heart so that you can see some of what He has in store for you.

Day 24

The Answered Prayer

"Then Eli answered and said,
'Go in peace, and the God of Israel grant your petition
which you have asked of Him.'"

(I Samuel 1:17)

During the course of this fast, you have petitioned God with specific requests, not only praying for your own deliverance, but interceding and seeking God on the behalf of your family and friends. Today, God has sent me to tell you that He hears you. Your prayers have not gone unheard, nor your surrender unnoticed, and many people will be blessed because of your sacrifice.

This morning as I prayed for my brother's salvation and for one marriage in particular, God lead me to I Samuel 1:17. It reads, "Then Eli said, Go in peace, and may the God of Israel grant your petition which you have asked of Him."

This is one of my favorite phrases in the Bible as it helped me through a challenging season in my life. My first pregnancy ended in a miscarriage and it was devastating. After that occurrence I was bombarded with negative thoughts: *Was I too old? Would I be able to conceive and carry a baby full-term? Was this punishment for some pass sin?* And as the fear grew, the questions increased.

In a quest for peace I turned to God's word and He directed me the book of 1 Samuel. The first few chapters feature the story of Hannah, a barren woman who desperately desired a son. So with a pure heart she cried out for God's help and He complied. By way of confirmation, Eli the priest spoke to her the scripture you read above (I Samuel 1:17). Those words were a huge source of comfort for Hannah and should be for us today.

The Word also tells us, *"For the eyes of the LORD are on the righteous, And His ears are open to their prayers* (1 Peter 3:12). Praise God! He hears our prayers and is ready to answer. What are you seeking God for? Ask in faith, according to His will, and it is done.

How do I know? Has He not requested that we *Let Him Do a New Thing*, and declared that we are to *Expect the Unexpected*? Has He not proclaimed that *It Will Come to Pass*, and that *Your Breakthrough is Coming Through*? What more can He say? As the prophet Eli instructed Hannah, "Go in peace." In other words be content with today, praise God for what He has already done, and wait expectantly, without worry, for what is to come.

Therefore, I am resting in the promises of God. I praise Him for my brother's salvation and the marriages that will be restored. I thank Him that I will be all that He has proclaimed within the next 16 days and the same can be true for you. Don't fret, it is already done, go in peace.

Personal Reflections

1. How is the Spirit speaking to you? Reflect on I Samuel 1:8-18 and journal your insights.

2. What specific requests have you put before God during the course of this fast? Do you believe that He will answer your prayers?

3. How is your thought life? During times of stress do you allow the enemy to bombard you with negative thoughts? Do you find solace in complaining? If you answered yes to either of those questions, what might you do differently the next time you are stressed about a particular situation?

Day 25

The Dead Will Live

*"As soon as Jesus heard the word that was spoken,
He said to the ruler of the synagogue,
'Do not be afraid; only believe.'"*

(Mark 5:36)

I can recall as a child hearing a preacher tell one unbelievable story of how he had been raised from the dead. Yes, you read correctly, raised from the dead.

This preacher was a sight to behold: tall, dark, and disfigured. His deformity, the result of a fire, had burned him across most of his body and subsequently killed him.

As a matter of fact, that would have been the end of the story, but God. Fortunately for him, there were many saints praying on his behalf. As a result of their prayers, he woke up in the morgue, naked, with a tag on his toe. Can you imagine the surprise, to put it mildly, of the attendant on duty that night?

In Jesus' day, a ruler of the synagogue came to Him by the name of Jairus. He prostrated himself at His feet, and begged that He come to lay hands on his little girl that was dying. Jesus agreed. Yet as they traveled, there were many distractions: the crowd, the woman with the issue of blood, and no doubt other requests of Jesus.

In no time, a servant reported that Jairus' daughter had died and that he should "cease from bothering and distressing the Teacher." For most people that would have been the end of the story: she's dead, it's over. But as the song reminds us, "It ain't over, until God says is over; He has the final say."

So the story continued. Jesus, having overhead the conversation between the ruler and his servant simply responded, "Do not be seized with alarm and struck with fear; only keep on believing" (Mark 5:36, Amplified Bible). With that, Jesus continued to Jairus' home, spoke to the little girl, and she lived.

What is your response to "dead" situations? Do you throw your hands up, give into the fear, and wallow in disappointment? Or do you pursue, with power, all that has been stolen from you? I pray it is the latter.

My friend, if God has spoken a thing to you in the spirit and your natural circumstances don't line up, so what! It's not over. Don't give into the fear and don't give up. Instead, pray with all your might, and praise God for what He has already done. The Word tells us to speak those things that are not as though they were so (see Romans 4:17). This is not the time for giving up but for establishing your faith.

Is there anyone better to put your faith in than Jesus? He, too, gave life to a dead situation. He was crucified, buried, and in three days resurrected. That miracle testifies to us today that our dead situations can also live if we only believe.

Rejoice because God has promised that he will restore the years that the locust has eaten—and that you, His people, will never be put to shame (see Joel 2:25-26). Therefore, in the next 15 days, let God resurrect and bring life to your dead situations.

Personal Reflections

1. How is the Spirit speaking to you? Reflect on Mark 5:21-43 and journal your insights.

2. We are all in need of prayer. Name the specific ways your accountability partner can pray for you this week then ask him/her to pray with you.

3. Can you recall a time when you thought all hope was lost yet God resurrected a dead situation in your life? What was that situation and how did God turn it around for you?

4. The Word says that if you faint in the day of adversity your strength is small (see Proverbs 24:10).

How do you handle adversity? Do you give up easily or forge ahead knowing that God has the final say?

5. Do you currently have a dead situation in your life? What is it? Do you believe that God can resurrect it?

Day 26

What is For Me is For Me

"He shall be like a tree
Planted by the rivers of water,
That brings forth its fruit in its season,
Whose leaf also shall not wither;
And whatever he does shall prosper."

(Psalm 1:3)

I was visiting a colleague's website last night and noticed that she had been asked to speak at a major event on the east coast. I immediately went to the event's webpage to see who else had been asked to speak. As I perused the site my mind started to spin; doubt threatened to consume me as one fear-based thought lead to another. My train of thought went something like this:

Why wasn't I asked to speak?; Because they don't know me; They don't know me because I am not connected to the right people; But how does one connect with the right people?; Perhaps if I was little less bible-based; Maybe if I watered the message down and made it more universally acceptable; Yes, I better change, otherwise I will never build a speaking platform and worse yet, life will pass me by.

Just thoughts, or are they? If they were *just* thoughts, then the scripture that directs us to bring "every thought into captivity to the obedience of Christ" would be unnecessary (2 Corinthians 10:5b). Our thoughts have power and if we linger on them long enough they'll direct our actions.

Therefore, as the thoughts attempted to bombard me, I did what I knew would bring relief—I fell on my knees and prayed to God for strength to challenge my thoughts. In an instant He comforted me with these words:

You can't miss out on what I have for you.

Those were the exact words that my prayer partner had spoken to me a few months prior and they brought me great comfort as I was reminded that *I can't miss out on what God has for me.*

The scripture tells us that the steps of a righteous man are ordered by the Lord (see Psalm 37:23). Because I am righteous (in right standing with God), habitually meditating on His word, and delighting myself in Him, I can't miss out! As the song goes, "What God has for me it is for me." Likewise, if you are in God's will, you can't miss out either. If He said it, it is so; His word will not return to Him void and it will achieve the purposes for which it was sent (see Isaiah 55:11).

Therefore when in despair, cling to these scriptures as your truth: "Delight yourself also in the LORD, And He shall give you the desires of your heart" (Psalm 37:4); and "If you diligently obey the voice of the LORD your God, to observe carefully all His commandments which I command you today, that the LORD your God will set you high above all nations of the earth. And all these blessings shall come upon you and overtake you, because you obey the voice of the LORD your God" (Deuteronomy 28:1-2). As my Auntie Gwen would say, "Those are words to live by."

Don't measure your life by the world's standards; don't let their timetables convince you that you are doing something wrong. God's timing is perfect and if you are walking in His will, He will bring forth the fruit of your labor in its season. I don't know about you, but I don't want what God hasn't ordained. While it might look good to the world its end is destruction.

Therefore, I praise God for reminding me and you that when we walk according to His plan we can't miss out. We can't miss connecting with the right people, finding the perfect job, being appointed over a ministry, elected into political office, finding the right mate, becoming a homeowner, or having children. Indeed, what He has me is or me and what he has for you is for you. Be encouraged!

Personal Reflections

1. How is the Spirit speaking to you? Reflect on 2 Corinthians 10:1-6 and journal your insights.

2. The mind is the battleground of the enemy. How often do you allow the enemy to have free reign of your thoughts? What will you do to gain better control over what you are thinking?

3. How confident are you that what God has for you is for you? Are there times when you compare yourself to others and become discouraged? How has God proven to you that His plan for you will come to pass?

4. List some of the promises that God has made to you. Thank Him for these promises and ask Him to give you peace as you patiently wait for the manifestation of His promises.

Day 27

Personal Time with God

SCRIPTURE(S):

HOW IS THE SPIRIT SPEAKING TO YOU?

Day 28

Personal Time with God

SCRIPTURE(S):

HOW IS THE SPIRIT SPEAKING TO YOU?

Day 29

The God of the Impossible

"But Jesus looked at them and said to them,
'With men this is impossible, but with God all things are possible.'"
(Matthew 19:26)

I have the ultimate praise report today! My brother, who I had declared would accept Christ as his personal savior before the conclusion of this fast, did. Yesterday, before hundreds of witnesses at my father's 10th Pastoral Anniversary Celebration in Lockport, New York, he received the gift of eternal salvation.

That is no small feat; God did the miraculous. My brother Stephen, age 27 and the youngest of us eight, was a tough sell; he didn't appear to have any interest in salvation. The rest of us had been saved for years, but not Stephen. He was content, or so he thought, to live his life in sin. But God always has the final say and He honors the prayers of His people.

I was later told that during the anniversary service my mother stood boldly before the people and announced that all of her children were saved. Stephen, sitting in the audience, probably thought, *you forgot about me*, but she hadn't. At that moment she was simply establishing her faith and God did the seemingly impossible in a matter of minutes.

How many times has God told you that He was going to move on your behalf or the behalf of your family and instead of proclaiming His declaration aloud, you sit on it till the enemy has convinced you otherwise? Certainly the scripture tells us there are times to have faith to ourselves but this is not for every instance. Sometimes God wants you to act in boldness and declare His promises aloud so that others will witness His mighty hand in your situation and also believe.

In this season, God is calling us to a level of radical faith that far exceeds our previous dealings with Him. He wants us to know that if He could part the Red Sea, feed 5,000 with two fish and five loaves of bread, and raise Jesus from the dead that He can *and* will move in our situations.

Will you not believe in Him today? He declares, "If you have faith as a mustard seed, you can say to this mulberry tree, 'Be pulled up by the roots and be planted in the sea,' and it would obey you" (Luke 17:6). Another scripture reads, "And whatever you ask in My name, that I will do, that the Father may be glorified in the Son. If you ask anything in My name, I will do *it*" (John 14:13-14).

Well I tell you I am inspired, my faith is strengthened and I am ready to make some more declarations according to the will of God and in the name of our Lord and Savior. Here are two more bold and courageous proclamations:

1. My brother's marriage will be restored by the conclusion of this fast. If you knew the story, this would sound like the impossible but God specializes

in things that are too difficult for man. I declare today that what is done in the spirit, will be manifested to us in the natural in the name of Jesus.

2. I will be debt free by the end of this calendar year (this includes my mortgage). I don't know how but last Sunday as I laid down for an afternoon nap, I whispered the same prayer I have whispered for the last two years, "Lord I thank you that we are debt free." And this time He added "this year." So in the name of Jesus, I declare that we are debt free in 2010.

I encourage you to pray, hear from God, and with holy boldness declare the humanly impossible. Some of you need college tuition, a wayward spouse to return home, a child to come off drugs, a spouse, promotion, new home, car, and/or God's peace; whatever it is, ask and BELIEVE. Better yet, why not DECLARE what God will do by sharing your belief with your accountability partner. Go ahead, you can do it! Act in faith and watch Him do beyond what you could ask or think. If He did it for us by saving our brother, He will also do it for you. Let it all be done in Jesus' name!

Personal Reflections

1. How is the Spirit speaking to you? Reflect on Matthew 19:23-30 and journal your insights.

2. What is faith? How has God tested your faith recently? What was the situation? Did the test draw you closer to God or cause you to move away. What do you need to do to increase you faith in God? What bold and courageous declarations will you make today? What impossible thing do you believe God will do for you?

3. Sometimes in our zeal we overstate God's will. How will you feel at the end of the fast if things don't turn about the way you envisioned? Will you still trust God to do the impossible?

Day 30

Little Time Needed

"For My thoughts are not your thoughts,
Nor are your ways My ways," says the LORD."

(Isaiah 55:8)

Today was unusual. I couldn't seem to get my thoughts together. I would start a blog post only to delete and start over. With each passing minute my anxiety grew. I feared that I wouldn't have time to write something meaningful. It was in that moment that the Holy Spirit whispered these profound words, *"God doesn't need a lot of time."* Take a moment and let that permeate into your being.

God doesn't need a lot of time.

Yesterday God asked us to declare in faith, and according to His will, what He will do for us; how He will bless us as a reward for our sacrifice. Some of you flat out refused. You weren't willing to put yourself "out there."

Although God has declared *new things* and for you to *expect the unexpected*, some of you continue to believe that these promises are for everyone else but you. Indeed for some of you that has been the story of your life: left out, forgotten and rejected. But not this time. He can and will do it for you in just 11 more days, if you step out in faith.

When I first started writing this blog, I wanted the posts to follow a succinct pattern. If I had had my way, each week would have covered a specific theme (e.g., Week 1-Fear; Week 2 – Self-esteem, etc.). But thank God He had another plan. As we are nearing the end, I realize that He has used this time to simply build our faith in Him.

The scripture reads in Jeremiah 17:5b, "Cursed is the man who trusts in man and makes flesh his strength, Whose heart departs from the LORD." We have learned and are continuing to learn, that our trust is to be in God, and Him alone; not other people or our own abilities. The latter is weak and leads to our doom, but when we trust in God, we trust in the source of all goodness and our success is guaranteed. He will do just as He said, in the amount of time that He chooses.

So let's start over. What has God declared that He will do for you by the conclusion of this fast? Then it is done. It is often for the building of your faith that He allows you to wait until His appointed time. Therefore, don't look at your circumstances just keep your eyes on God. I don't care if you are in the 11th hour, if He said He will do it, it is done. Remember, He doesn't need a lot of time so simply believe and receive your inheritance.

Personal Reflections

1. How is the Spirit speaking to you? Reflect on Jeremiah 17:5-8 and journal your insights.

2. Yesterday's blog post asked you to write down what you believe God will do for you before this fast's end. Did you do that? If not, what stopped you from making a declaration?

3. The old saying goes, "He may not come when you want, but He is always on time." Do you believe this to be true? Can you recall a time when you thought all hope was gone? Did things eventually work out for you? What lessons did you learn from that particular circumstance?

Day 31

Grace and Glory

*"For by grace you have been saved through faith,
and that not of yourselves;
it is the gift of God, not of works, lest anyone should boast."*

(Ephesians 2:8-9)

We are in the last quarter of this race. I pray that you remain focused so that you are able to win and receive all that God has for you!

Last night in Bible Study the praise team sang a song that continues to permeate my spirit. The lyrics, *"All the glory belongs to you, All the glory belongs to you, O God"* are on my lips even this morning. For indeed, all the glory belongs to God for what He has done and will do.

I am specifically praising God this morning for His grace. Grace is God's unmerited favor and the power to do what we can't do in our own strength. When we accepted Christ as our personal savior, it was God's grace that made it possible. The writer Paul wrote:

"But God, who is rich in mercy, because of His great love with which He loved us, even when we were dead in trespasses, made us alive together with

Christ (by grace you have been saved)," (Ephesians 2:4-5).

Without God's grace we would still be dead in our sins, wallowing in a sea of defeat and desperation.

So why then as believers are we living in a state of virtual gracelessness; not allowing Him to work on our behalf? Indeed, if we needed Him then (to receive the gift of salvation), we need Him now. It is only by His grace that we will accomplish what He wills for our lives and succeed.

I told you in a former post that I was uncomfortable with writing. So when God called me to blog, I knew I needed His grace and power to do what was outside of my skill-set and comfort level. Therefore, each morning I submit to His plan, listen for what He has to say, and write as He instructs. And look what He has done! Many of you (including readers from 10 different countries) have been blessed by God's grace operating in my life.

I sense that some of you are working too hard for God's dream. He has promised you "X" and before He can work on your behalf, you are making futile efforts to make it so. God doesn't need your help; it is not by your works that His will comes to pass, but His grace. I heard Pastor Paul Sheppard say, "When we fight, God doesn't." This isn't to imply that we are to live passively, it's simply a reminder that God is in control and we are to move only as He leads.

Therefore, if God has promised to save your son, stop lecturing him. If God has promised to bring your husband into right fellowship with Him, stop criticizing him. If God has promised to give you a new car, don't settle for a used one. Stand on His word, get out of the way, and let Him work!

Indeed God will do a great work by the end of this fast and His grace will allow His every promise to come true for you. If your faith is lacking, re-read the post entitled, *Rebuild and Renew*. It reminds you that God is looking to bless you and your families outrageously as a result of your sacrifice. All He needs for you to do is to believe and let His grace flow.

Take courage. Speak aloud what God has promised He will do. If you don't know what that is, ask. The scripture reads, "If any of you lacks wisdom, let him ask of God, who gives to all liberally and without reproach, and it will be given to him" (James 1:5). And when He gives you His plan, believe it. Refrain from planning how you will make it happen; simply let His grace and His power direct your every step.

To God be the glory. I can't wait to hear the testimonies of how His grace empowered you to do what you were unable to do in your own strength; how your surrender has made the impossible, possible.

Now sing with me, "All the glory belongs to you, All the glory belongs to you, O God."

Personal Reflections

1. How is the Spirit speaking to you? Reflect on Ephesians 2:1-10 and journal your insights.

2. As the song implies, "All the glory belongs to God." What does that mean to you? Take a moment to write down one thing God has done for you in the last week; the last month; and the last year.

3. Are you one to allow God's grace to operate in your life or do you try to do most things in your own strength?

4. Have you or are you now in God's way? Identify how.

5. For which challenging situations do you need to leave more room for God's grace to operate? What will you do so that God has complete control?

Day 32

ACT LIKE YOU ARE ABOUT TO MOVE

"Pass through the camp and command the people, saying,
'Prepare provisions for yourselves, for within three days you will
cross over this Jordan, to go in to possess the land which the LORD
your God is giving you to possess.'"

(Joshua 1:11)

There was a message preached by Pastor John K. Jenkins, Sr. of the First Baptist Church of Glenarden that left a lasting impression on me. Ironically, I can't recall the theme of the message or even the sermon title but one key point stuck out for me. He said that faith is active and when God has spoken a word in your life, act as if it is already done.

I was speaking with a sister who shared with me that God has promised her a new home at a specific address. I readily replied, "start acting like you are about to move." My instructions to her included:

1. ***Purge the junk.*** Throw out those things that are not suitable for your new dwelling place.

2. ***Scout out the land.*** Go to the new address and pray over your new home and neighborhood.

3. ***Prepare for transport.*** Phone moving companies, compare rates, and decide which company to use.

In other words, ACT LIKE YOU ARE ABOUT TO MOVE.

If God has promised you a new car, start visiting dealerships to learn everything there is to know about the car buying process. If God has promised to send you to school, start scouting the local colleges; learn which have your major, and who will fund you. If God has promised you a promotion, learn all that you need to know about your next position. If God has promised you a husband, get out the house and move in circles that are husband-friendly so he can find you!

In other words, ACT LIKE YOU ARE ABOUT TO MOVE.

There is a period of time late in a woman's pregnancy where she actively prepares for her baby's arrival. No matter how long her journey or how challenging the pregnancy, every expectant mother comes to this stage. It's called Nesting. It is in this stage that she finds renewed energy and strength to prepare for her impending blessing. In fact, it has been reported that nurseries have been completed in a day by the pregnant woman alone! In that instance she was acting like she was about to move.

Lately, I've been hearing the words, *start acting like you are a business.* Although everything around me doesn't look like a business (e.g., I am still typing a blog from my family room), I am heeding these words. Accordingly, I have contacted a web designer, researched speaker agents, and developed a plan for hiring staff. Hey, it may not look like it right now but I am giving birth to an international ministry of ginormous proportion.

What dream(s) are you about to birth? It doesn't matter how long you have waited or how challenging the journey, moving day is here and by faith it is done.

Have you heard the term, "Fake it 'til you make it?" Well that's what we're doing. It might not look like it right now but our change is here: we are business owners, husbands, wives, parents of successful children, philanthropists, award-winning artists, teachers, lawyers, chefs, and pastors. Our marriages thrive, our family members are saved, and we are well—mind, body, and spirit. And this is all possible because we have surrendered our collective wills for God's. Now He is ready to act on our behalf.

Therefore, step out in faith; prepare your provisions, and ACT LIKE YOU ARE ABOUT TO MOVE.

Personal Reflections

1. How is the Spirit speaking to you? Reflect on Joshua 1:10-18 and journal your insights.

2. What does the phrase ACT LIKE YOU ARE ABOUT TO MOVE mean to you?

3. It is said that preparation plus opportunity equals success. Think of one dream that God has placed in your heart. In what ways are you preparing for the manifestation of that dream?

4. What signs have God shown you to let you know that He is ready to work on your behalf?

DAY 33

The Promise

*"And everyone who has left houses
or brothers or sisters or father or mother or wife or children or lands,
for My name's sake, shall receive a hundredfold, and inherit
eternal life."*

(Matthew 19:29)

Exodus 20:2-3 reads, "I *am* the LORD your God, who brought you out of the land of Egypt, out of the house of bondage. You shall have no other gods before Me."

Those words, first spoken to the children of Israel after their exodus from Egypt, are still relevant today. We are to put nothing before God because He can and will meet all of our needs. There is nothing that can replace the love, joy, and peace that following Him brings. And lest we forget that truth, He tests us.

Throughout history, God has tested the allegiance of His people. Abraham was commanded to sacrifice His son Isaac—the product of this old age and key to the fulfillment of God's promises to him. Ruth chose to stay with Naomi her widowed mother-in-law, rather than pursue a seemingly better life among her people. Queen Esther, who had at her disposal all the luxuries that life could offer, risked her life to save God's people from destruction. Because of their obedience, their sacrifices were rewarded handsomely; God manifested His glory and blessed them beyond what they would have gained had they acted selfishly. In other words, their sacrifices reaped a hundredfold harvest.

Likewise, we are of this number; we are also the blessed. Some 33 days ago, in a radical act of obedience we responded to God's challenge and surrendered what was dear to us; what we thought sustained our very existence. Collectively we have sacrificed our idols—food, free-time, cowardice, timidity, unforgiveness, and control—to God, and have pursued Him with all our might.

God has said throughout the course of this fast that our sacrifices have not gone unnoticed. He now promises that He will render a hundredfold blessing; a blessing, in fact, that is exceedingly abundantly above all that we ask or think (see Ephesians 3:20).

It has been a pleasure to be on this journey with you. As we embark upon our last week, let us not neglect to reflect on how far God has brought us. I don't know about you, but I am a different person. The idols of timidity and cowardice have been replaced with courage and boldness, but it is not over yet. I look forward to what God will do for us on next week.

Lastly, God has given us a powerful word this week. To summarize, here's His promise: "I am the God of the impossible; miracles are my specialty and I don't need a lot of time to perform them. If you would allow my grace to empower your every action, I will get the glory, and you will receive all that I have promised, even a hundredfold." Amen.

Personal Reflections

1. How is the Spirit speaking to you? Reflect on Matthew 19:23-30 and journal your insights.

2. What sacrifices have you made in the past? In what way(s) did God reward you for your sacrifice(s)?

3. Are there people or situations that you put before God? If yes, who are they and what will you do to make this right?

4. How do you feel about there being one last week? Has this process helped you to feel closer to God? Have you noticed changes in yourself and others? List those changes here.

Day 34

Personal Time with God

SCRIPTURE(S):

HOW IS THE SPIRIT SPEAKING TO YOU?

Day 35

Personal Time with God

SCRIPTURE(S):

HOW IS THE SPIRIT SPEAKING TO YOU?

DAY 36

No More Props

"FOR BEHOLD, the Lord, the Lord of hosts, is taking away from Jerusalem
and from Judah the stay and the staff [every kind of prop],
the whole stay of bread and the whole stay of water,"

(Isaiah 3:1, Amplified Bible)

My Aaliyah, soon to be four years old, has times when she wants to be a baby again, especially when she's feeling frightened. In a futile attempt to regress, she asks for items that represent her babyhood, like a sippy cup or a stroller. When this occurs, AJ, her six-year-old, know-it-all brother, cries out in frustration, "You are not a baby anymore!" In those moments the truth of his declaration is unsettling for her. I can see the agitation on her face as she attempts to embrace her new reality: *I am a big girl now.*

This truth, *I am a big girl/boy now*, can also be unsettling for the believer. As babes in Christ, He gives us all sorts of baby items or "props" that enable us to succeed. These props can include new member's classes, extensive guidance from godly mentors, and affiliation with certain beginner-type ministries, yet there comes a time when we have to grow up. It is then that He removes every prop and requires us to stand on our own. This season can be scary, but the Holy Spirit, our comforter, is right there to guide and gently remind us that we are no longer babes in Christ.

By way of this prop-removing process, I have gone from a babe in the faith to a budding powerhouse. At the top of this year, God required that I drop most every activity that brought me a sense of fulfillment. He isolated me and begun the process of my knowing Him for myself. The first thing that He did was reveal to me a startling truth: I had grown far too reliant on other people's faith. I had become accustomed to depending on others to tell me what God was saying, but now that needed to be my responsibility.

For example, my parents, pillars of faith, had been one of my props. Whenever a crisis arose I would run straight to them. When I was diagnosed with cancer, my mother's prophesy "this is not until death" fueled my faith. When my friend suffered a stroke, my Dad's words, "she will fully recover," fueled our faith. But now God is saying *No More.* He has removed every prop and now I have to hear God for myself and speak just as He instructs. I must admit it's kind of frightening, yet necessary for my growth.

Amazingly, I woke up this morning humming the song "Jesus is Real," by Pastor John P. Kee. The lyrics, "Jesus is real, I know the Lord is real to me," played over and over in my head. That is now my truth. My prayer partner had prophesied some months back that this was the season for us to "see God." I didn't understand then, but now I do. God has removed every prop so that I can see and know Him for myself.

Perhaps you are experiencing a similar experience and God has removed all your props. If so, you will no longer be able to depend on your parents, pastor, TV evangelist, ministry leaders and mentors for a word. He is requiring that you to know His voice for yourself.

Paul wrote, "When I was a child, I spoke as a child, I understood as a child, I thought as a child; but when I became a man, I put away childish things" (I Corinthians 13:11).

Depending solely on other people to hear a word from God is childish. It is time that we hear, believe, and speak God's truth as He has spoken it to us. We need not be afraid; we need not regress to our babyhood in Christ. The props have been removed and in their place lay supernatural faith that will turn this world upside down.

Personal Reflections

1. How is the Spirit speaking to you? Reflect on Isaiah 3:1 and I Corinthians 13:11 and journal your insights.

2. What are the props that are in your life?

3. A benefit of releasing your props is the ability to hear God for yourself and to have a closer, more intimate relationship with Him. Is God telling you that it is time to let Him remove the props? Are you willing to let go? Why or why not?

4. What do you anticipate your life will be like without the props?

Day 37

Reject Rejection

"Whoever listens to you listens to me; whoever rejects you rejects me; but whoever rejects me rejects him who sent me."

(Luke 10:16)

During His public ministry, Jesus chose and appointed seventy men to go two by two into every town and place, where He Himself would eventually enter, to minister the good news of the gospel (see Luke 10:1). He urged them to be productive and to operate according to the authority given to them.

The seventy did as instructed. With passion they preached "the kingdom of God is at hand," with authority they cast out demons, and without provocation they spoke blessings over those who received them and warnings to those who did not. Even in the face of outright rejection they wouldn't fear or change the message; they simply kicked the dust off their feet and moved on.

My father accepted Christ when I was six years old. He and his radical Christian friends were on-fire for God, and didn't mind letting the world know. In their zeal—and to my horror—they started a street ministry. My friends would ask, "Didn't I see your father preaching on the corner?" I would quickly deny I knew such a man. But yes, it was my father and his friends preaching on the streets.

Despite the rejection, which was great, they were fearless. Passersby would cross to the other side, roll their eyes, plug their ears and verbally fight their message, yet they weren't deterred. They understood, as we should today, that the rejection was not about them, but Christ. Through it all they learned to reject rejection.

Rejecting rejection is not innate. Everything in us screams that we should avoid rejection at all cost, but today we are being instructed to reject rejection.

You may not have a street ministry like my Dad or find yourself going from place to place like the seventy, but you do have an obligation to preach the good news of the gospel to those around you, by word and deed. Don't fret if family, friends, and/or co-workers are less than thrilled with the "new" you who has emerged as a result of this fast. My friend, that just comes with the territory. No matter what, simply tell them the truth of God's word and if they reject it, shake the dust off your feet and keep moving.

I truly hope you realize that you are different as a result of this fast; no one can have an encounter with God and remain unchanged. Therefore, be about your Father's business and do what He requires. He will use you to call into existence that which is not, to move mountains in faith, and to draw men to Him. Over time you will have the same testimony as the seventy, who reported to Jesus, "Lord, even the demons are subject to us in Your name." Praise God that we have all authority over the enemy so there is nothing to fear. Therefore, keep the faith, do as instructed, and learn to reject rejection.

Personal Reflections

1. How is the Spirit speaking to you? Reflect on Luke
   10:1-20 and journal your insights.

2. How do you handle rejection? Are you easily
   wounded by another's rejection or can you shake it
   off and move on? If the former, how will the
   scriptures in Luke 10 help you to better deal with
   rejection?

3. Do you sense God calling you to do something
   radical like Dr. Celeste's dad? What is it? Will you
   be obedient to God's command?

4. Isn't being reminded that the demons are subject to Jesus encouraging? Will this truth allow you to release fear so that you are better able to follow God's commands no matter the potential for rejection?

5. In which area of your life will you work on releasing fear?

Day 38

Childlike Humility

"Therefore, whoever takes the lowly position of this child is the greatest in the kingdom of heaven."

(Matthew 18:4)

It occurred to me this morning that God is ministering His final instructions to us. Monday: *No More Props*; yesterday: *Reject Rejection*, and today: *Childlike Humility*. For that reason, "He who has an ear, let him hear what the Spirit says to the churches" (Revelations 2:17).

At the top of Matthew 18, Jesus' disciples came to Him and asked, "Who then is greatest in the kingdom of heaven?" Jesus, in typical fashion, delivered His answer through demonstration. He called to Himself a child and said, "Assuredly, I say to you, unless you are converted and become as little children, you will by no means enter the kingdom of heaven" (Matthew 18:3).

As believers we know that we are destined for heaven, but the kingdom that Jesus speaks of in Matthew 18 is God's kingdom here on earth. Each of us has been bestowed a kingdom often called "destiny" which is our place of assignment. Our arrival to this place is determined by God, but also contingent on our mindset. Without the proper mindset we will never arrive. Take the children of Israel for example. Their complaining and arrogance robbed them of the opportunity to inhabit the land flowing with milk and honey.

The destiny mindset is one of total surrender and complete humility. The word humility is derived from the word humble which means not proud or haughty. When one is humble he lives a life of submission and considers himself low in a hierarchy. He isn't vying for position, stepping on others to advance and merely concentrating on his own needs. No, the humble believer is like a child.

Children are amazing to watch. I have the pleasure of parenting two wonderful little gifts. Unfortunately, there are times when they behave improperly and must be chastised. Even then...one minute they are crying and angry, but the next lowly and apologetic, as they hug me about the legs.

That is what our heavenly father requires of us: a complete surrender and trust of His plan. He isn't looking for the smartest and the brightest, or requiring us to have degrees and other achievements, for surely "the last will be first, and the first last." He simply seeks whom He can use for the edifying and building of His kingdom.

This fast has been about exercising a spirit of humility; about ridding ourselves of the hindrances that keep us from being all that God requires. It hasn't been easy but well worth the effort. Ironically enough, we started this fast with a discussions on humility (see *Expect the Unexpected*) and ending with the same. It is clear that we need humility to be all that God has called us to be.

Lastly, I thank God for His purging process. We are now better equipped for kingdom work because we have exercised, through surrender, childlike humility.

Personal Reflections

1. How is the Spirit speaking to you? Reflect on Matthew 18:1-5 and journal your insights.

2. How is surrendering your will a demonstration of humility?

3. Why do you think humility is so important to God? In which areas of your life could you exercise more humility.

4. Humility is necessary for us to be in healthy relationships. Romans 12:3 reads, "For I say, through the grace given to me, to everyone who is among you, not to think of himself more highly than he ought to think, but to think soberly, as God has dealt to each one a measure of faith." How do you think having humility in your relationships will strengthen them?

Day 39

Wait on the Lord

"So I will restore to you the years that the swarming locust has eaten,
The crawling locust,
The consuming locust,
And the chewing locust,
My great army which I sent among you.
You shall eat in plenty and be satisfied,
And praise the name of the LORD your God,
Who has dealt wondrously with you;
And My people shall never be put to shame."

(Joel 2:25-26)

At 61, my dad is in the prime of His life. He is the husband of Malinda, his bride of 41 years, the father to 8 saved children, grandfather to 12, the Pastor of 2 churches, the Superintendent/Overseer for 4 other churches, the owner of a lovely home and two luxury vehicles.

It hasn't always been that way; growing up, finances were tight. My dad, the sole bread-winner, was often in and out of work. All ten of us shared a three bedroom home with one bath. The church van was often our primary mode of transport. We always had dinner, but I know there were times when my parents weren't sure how the Lord would provide. We used food stamps, ate government cheese, and wore hand-me-downs (well at least my siblings did, one of the perks of being the oldest was that I was able to wear each item first!).

Regardless of the challenges he faced, my dad never allowed the circumstances to deter him from his proper position in the home; he always gave his family his best. All the while God was watching and storing up his blessings.

At the same time, my dad was an associate minister with a local congregation. He sat under that leadership for many years. While others would've been itching to get their own church, my dad was unwilling to move without God's leading. All the while God was watching and storing up his blessings.

My dad was in poor health in his 40s. At 42, his mother died of a massive heart attack. Accordingly, he had his first heart attack at 42 and a few years later another. Yet again, he remained faithful. All the while God was watching and storing up his blessings.

Needless to say, the locust had eaten a lot, and things didn't look good—but God; He is never slack concerning His promises. Over those years God had spoken many wonderful blessings over my Dad's life—that he would have a beautiful home, he would place in him a new (physical) heart, and that he would pastor many. Because His word will not return to Him void, those promises had to come to pass. Although my dad's circumstances often looked bleak, he chose to believe God. Now his faith is being rewarded and he is enjoying the fruit of his labor and basking in God's overflow. As promised, God has restored all the years the locust had eaten and my Dad is not ashamed.

Maybe you can only relate to the first portion of my Dad's story. Maybe you're struggling, unsure of God's plan, and growing weary with each passing day. Well don't give up. God is watching and storing up your blessings.

Today, my dad and mom are shining examples of what waiting on the Lord looks like. Because God is faithful; He has restored them completely and they are being drenched in His latter rain. In fact, He is preparing them for even more, including international ministry. Who says God can't make up for (what we perceive as) lost time? He can and will restore!

As God has said repeatedly during the course of this fast, your surrender has not gone unnoticed. Your willingness to submit to His plan for these last 39 days has caused Him to store blessings on your behalf. You may be seeing some of the benefits now, but that's only the beginning. You have an abundant harvest waiting on you, so don't give up.

Wait on the Lord and be of good courage. You will bask in the overflow and reap an abundant harvest if you faint not. No matter what the locust has eaten or stolen, God will restore it ALL and you will not be put to shame. Amen.

Personal Reflections

1. How is the Spirit speaking to you? Reflect on I Kings 8:56; Joshua 21:45; and Joel 2:18-27 and journal your insights.

2. God will restore all that the locust has eaten. What area(s) of your life are in need of repair and restoration?

3. During the course of this fast, how has God made changes in your circumstances?

4. How do you see God continuing to restore over the course this year? In five years? In ten years?

Day 40

God Has Done a New Thing

Welcome to Day 40! What a journey this has been. You may recall that we started this journey with these words: *Let God Do a New Thing* and thus appropriately ending with this phrase: *God Has Done a New Thing*.

God told us from the beginning to simply give Him 40 days and a surrendered heart and He would change our lives. I praise Him for what He has done! The song, *Marvelous* by the late Bishop Walter Hawkins is ringing in my spirit:

> *I will sing your praise*
> *for you've done such a Marvelous thing.*
> *For someone so wretched*
> *yet my soul you have redeemed*
>
> *No one else could do it.*
> *No one could care half as much.*
> *Yet you thought my soul was worth it.*
> *So you gave your only son.*
>
> *You gave that I might live.*

You gave that I might be set free.
Exchanged your life for mine.
What a Marvelous thing you've done.

I am appropriately silenced this morning. I simply hear God saying, "Oh, give thanks to the LORD" (Psalm 105:1a)! Take the time this morning and throughout the weekend to reflect on what God has done during these 40-days. I pray that you have allowed Him to do a new thing in you. Be blessed!

CONCLUSION

It's been nearly a year since I wrote that blog, yet each time I read it I am encouraged all over again. Likewise, I continue to get emails and phone calls from other fasters who report that they, too, are seeing the benefits of their surrender.

On another note, you may be wondering about Day 29 and those last two bold and courageous declarations. Well things did not turn out the way I desired. My brother's marriage dissolved and I was not debt-free at the close of 2010. I was bummed to say the least.

As a matter of fact, while developing this text for publication I seriously contemplated deleting those two declarations. I couldn't even read them without cringing and certainly didn't want you, the reader, to know how badly I had messed up. But you know what? Life happens and sometimes in our zeal we misspeak. I wish I could say it won't ever happen again, but I can't...I'm human. However, on the flip side we can be comforted by this truth: God judges the heart (not the mistake) and rewards accordingly. I believe He knew I had the best intentions when I spoke those declarations and I also believe He is continuing to honor my faith, albeit naïve and misguided.

Ironically, mistakes teach us a lot about God and life. I learned from my blooper to be careful about saying, "God said." As a result, I diligently watching my words and reframe from taking His name in vain by declaring that He said something He did not say. Again, can I say I will always get it right from here on out? Of course not! But I will try my best. Remember…a closer walk with God, not perfection, is the goal.

Please let me know how the Surrender Fast has blessed you. I can be reached on either of my websites: www.DrCelesteOwens.com or www.SurrenderFast.com. All the best to you and I am wishing you God's good success in every area of your life!

ABOUT THE AUTHOR

Dr. Celeste Owens is dedicated to enriching the lives of others. Her mission is to motivate and inspire every person to succeed. Because she believes that every person was created for a specific purpose and has the potential to succeed beyond measure, she gives tirelessly of her gifts and talents.

Dr. Celeste has not always been so confident about her place in the world. As a child she thought she was irrelevant and often longed to be someone else or dead. Her young adulthood reflected this inner turmoil and she made many mistakes. Her wake-up call came in the form of an automobile accident. That accident began for her the journey back to the person God intended for her to be from the beginning. After several years of soul-searching, she began to believe that God intended to use her as His vessel to change the world. She then became excited, not only about her life, but the lives of others. Now she is on a mission to help everyone realize their worth. Her desire is to see every person embrace their life and fulfill the destiny for which God has created them.

Dr. Celeste's speaking career began in 2004 as a faculty member with the University of Maryland at Baltimore. Today, she has gained national respect and attention for her thought-provoking presentations. Her impassioned approach to life and accomplishments as a psychologist and writer has made her a popular speaker for government agencies, churches, and community organizations. An expert on personal growth and trauma, she has appeared on cable television, and featured in local and national press including the Washington Post. She is an avid writer whose columns appear in various online magazines. Her blog *The Good Success Movement* is receiving excellent reader and viewer reviews.

Dr. Celeste's education includes a B.A. in Psychology from the State University of New York at Buffalo, a M.S. in Applied Counseling Psychology from the University of Baltimore and a Ph.D. in Counseling Psychology from the University of Pittsburgh.

In her spare time, she is actively involved in her local church and various other service organizations where she volunteers her time and talents generously. Dr. Celeste resides in the surrounding Washington Metropolitan Area where her most important works are being wife to her husband of more than 10 years and mom to their two young children.